CONSTRUCTIONS OF NEUROSCIENCE IN EARLY CHILDHOOD EDUCATION

This book explores and critiques topical debates in educational sciences, philosophy, social work and cognitive neuroscience. It examines constructions of children, parents and the welfare state in relation to neurosciences and its vocabulary of brain architecture, critical periods and toxic stress.

The authors provide insight into the historical roots of the relationship between early childhood education policy and practice and sciences. The book argues that the neurophilia in the early childhood education field is not a coincidence, but relates to larger societal changes that value economic arguments over ethical, social and eminently pedagogical concerns. It affects the image of the child, the parent and the very meaning of education in general.

Constructions of Neuroscience in Early Childhood Education discusses what neuroscience has to offer, what its limitations are and how to gain a more nuanced view on its benefits and challenges. The debates in this book will support early childhood researchers, students and practitioners in the field to make their own judgements about new evolutions in the scientific discourse.

Michel Vandenbroeck is head of the Department of Social Work and Social Pedagogy at Ghent University.

CONTESTING EARLY CHILDHOOD

Series Editors: Liselott Mariett Olsson and Michel Vandenbroeck

This groundbreaking series questions the current dominant discourses surrounding early childhood, and offers instead alternative narratives of an area that is now made up of a multitude of perspectives and debates.

The series examines the possibilities and risks arising from the accelerated development of early childhood services and policies, and illustrates how it has become increasingly steeped in regulation and control. Insightfully, this collection of books shows how early childhood services can in fact contribute to ethical and democratic practices. The authors explore new ideas taken from alternative working practices in both the western and developing world, and from other academic disciplines such as developmental psychology. Current theories and best practice are placed in relation to the major processes of political, social, economic, cultural and technological change occurring in the world today.

Titles in the *Contesting Early Childhood* series include:

CONSTRUCTIONS OF NEUROSCIENCE IN EARLY CHILDHOOD EDUCATION

Michel Vandenbroeck with Jan De Vos, Wim Fias, Liselott Mariett Olsson, Helen Penn, Dave Wastell and Sue White

Routledge
Taylor & Francis Group

LONDON AND NEW YORK

First published 2017
by Routledge
2 Park Square, Milton Park, Abingdon, Oxon OX14 4RN

and by Routledge
711 Third Avenue, New York, NY 10017

Routledge is an imprint of the Taylor & Francis Group, an informa business

British Library Cataloguing in Publication Data
A catalogue record for this book is available from the British Library

Library of Congress Cataloging in Publication Data
Names: Vandenbroeck, Michel, editor.
Title: Constructions of neuroscience in early childhood education / edited by Michel Vandenbroeck.
Description: Abingdon, Oxon ; New York, NY : Routledge, 2017. |
Series: Contesting early childhood
Identifiers: LCCN 2016056825 | ISBN 9781138214811 (hardback) |
ISBN 9781138214828 (pbk.) | ISBN 9781315445120 (ebook)
Subjects: LCSH: Cognitive learning. | Cognitive neuroscience. | Cognition in children. | Early childhood education.
Classification: LCC LB1062 .C658 2017 | DDC 370.15/23--dc23
LC record available at https://lccn.loc.gov/2016056825

ISBN: 978-1-138-21481-1 (hbk)
ISBN: 978-1-138-21482-8 (pbk)
ISBN: 978-1-315-44512-0 (ebk)

Typeset in Bembo
by Taylor & Francis Books

MIX
Paper from
responsible sources
FSC
www.fsc.org   FSC™ C013985

Printed in the United Kingdom
by Henry Ling Limited

CONTENTS

CONTRIBUTORS

Jan De Vos, MA in psychology and PhD in philosophy, works as a postdoctoral researcher at the Department of Philosophy and Moral Science at Ghent University (Belgium). He works on the critique of (neuro)psychology, (neuro)psychologisation and, related to this, the subject of the digital turn. He has published widely on these topics, including *The metamorphoses of the brain – Neurologisation and its discontents* (Palgrave, 2016), *Neuroscience and critique. Exploring the limits of the neurological turn* (Routledge, 2015), *Psychologization and the subject of late modernity* (Palgrave, 2014) and *Psychologisation in times of globalisation* (Routledge, 2012).

Wim Fias obtained his PhD in Experimental Psychology at KULeuven. He is now full professor of Experimental Psychology at Ghent University, where he holds the Chair of the Multidisciplinary Research Platform of Neuroscience and is co-chairing the Institute for Neuroscience. He teaches neuropsychology and cognitive neuroscience. Using behavioural and neuroimaging research techniques in a complementary way, he investigates the neural basis of mathematical cognition, memory, attention and cognitive control.

Liselott Mariett Olsson is Senior Lecturer in Pedagogy and Coordinator of the Early Childhood Teacher Education programme at Södertörn University, Stockholm, Sweden. Departing from her experiences as a preschool teacher, she authored a dissertation in pedagogy that focused on philosophical perspectives on sense and subjectivity in young children's learning. She is the author of *Movement and experimentation in young children's learning: Deleuze and Guattari in early childhood education*, which was published in the series *Contesting Early Childhood* that she now co-edits with Michel Vandenbroeck.

Helen Penn was a Director of Children's Services in Scotland, then became a senior researcher at the Institute of Education (IoE), University College London. Subsequently she was Professor of Early Childhood, and Professor Emerita at the University of East London. She is shortly to return to IoE as a Visiting Professor. She has had a long time interest in development aid issues and has undertaken work for a variety of international organizations including EU, OECD, UNICEF, UNESCO and Save the Children. Her new book, *Early childhood: Interpreting theories, approaches, policies and practice in development work*, is co-edited with Anne-Trine Kjorholt from the Norwegian Childhood Research Centre and will be published in 2018 by Palgrave Macmillan.

Michel Vandenbroeck is head of the Department of Social Work and Social Pedagogy at Ghent University, Belgium. After some 30 years of conducting innovation projects in the field of early childhood education, he made a PhD on a genealogy of child care in Belgium. His research is on family policies and early childhood education with a particular focus on issues of diversity and processes of inclusion and exclusion. He co-edits the series *Contesting Early Childhood* with Liselott Mariett Olsson.

Dave Wastell spent the first stage of his research career as a neuroscientist, completing his PhD at Durham University before taking up a lectureship at Manchester Medical School. He subsequently moved into Information Systems, gaining a chair at Salford University in 1999. Following a short period at Manchester University, he moved to Nottingham University Business School in 2004, retiring in 2014 as Emeritus Professor of Information Systems.

Sue White is Professor of Social Work at the University of Sheffield. Her research has focused principally on the detailed sociological analysis of everyday professional decision-making in child health and welfare. She is currently examining the impacts of technological biology on social policy and public discourse.

PREFACE

Liselott Mariett Olsson and Michel Vandenbroeck

> There is only one general principle in ethics: no process-line has the God-given 'right' to tell another one to 'wink out'. Constituencies interested in annihilation should be graciously encouraged to go first to show how it is done: to make an example of themselves by 'winking' out before they do ecological harm to other forms of life. Ethics is exemplary.
>
> *(Massumi, 2002: 256)*

This book is the first book that we, as new editors for the series *Contesting Early Childhood*, have published. It is a "severe" book that delivers sharp critique of one current phenomenon in early childhood education and care, the translation of neuroscience into education. However, the book is "severe" for a purpose. The ways in which early childhood education are viewed and shaped have, since its origins, always been contingent with the social economic and political contexts. Early childhood education is indeed a place where the political (i.e. ideas on what a "good life" is and on the role of the state in this) is confronted with the intimacy of the daily life of children, parents and teachers. It needs, therefore, to be a democratic place par excellence, a place where the meaning of "a good life" can be continuously contested and discussed by all who are concerned. However, we live in a period where there seems to be only one logic prevailing – a single individualistic, economic, meritocratic and, not the least, abstract logic. In that world view, this includes a specific image of the child, parental responsibility, and the purpose of education, science and the neurosciences in particular play a pivotal role. When neuro-scientific translation joins market-force interference and bureaucratic formalism, this may add to the construction of hostile identity-politics in early childhood. Hence, there is the need for criticism and response.

Despite this, this is not a book that wants to "do away" with science in general and neuroscience in particular, nor to close the doors for what might come out of neuroscience and early childhood in the future. It is more like a cry of warning in times where it seems more important than ever before to keep a multitude of ideas alive and communicating, not the least "old" ideas of early childhood education and care that might have much to say even today. We can make our contemporary problems speak with history in a way that what today seems "new" may come forward as just a new appearance of a much older problem. Or in ways that question if newer is always better (or always worse, for that matter). But we may also revisit history in order to gain insights that might help us reformulate and reinvent our contemporary problems. Often, the most important thing is not how we respond to problems but rather how we pose them. Here, history can help us navigate in our contemporary setting with some additional understanding of the ethical importance of a multitude of discourses as well as the necessity to engage in a continuous effort to create new ones.

Even though the contributions in this book mainly deal with a theory and policy perspective on the issue at stake, we believe that the book should be read also as a very concrete description of a certain "state of affairs" in early childhood practices. Our hopes are that the book can also function as a sort of "tool-box" for practitioners, a set of counter-arguments to be used when one feels that one's practice is being hi-jacked by a logic that does not benefit the purpose of raising and educating young children in democratic practices. Indeed, one thing is very clear in the present-day hegemony of the brain discourse in early childhood education: practitioners and researchers should not be considered as mere consumers of the hegemonic discourse. Discourse is what is made by all of us, and thus, it is also what can be contested and *re*-made by all of us. Therefore, we do not consider this contribution to the series as a mere "Contesting" book. It is not just *against* something (in casu the abuse of neuroscience and its functions in a meritocratic society). It is also *for* a cause: the cause of pedagogy.

Pedagogy, in our view, is not about the mere implementation of some knowledge from psychology, sociology, neuroscience or other sciences in the educational field. Pedagogy is about the use of knowledge and scholarly insights that have been built within this knowledge-tradition long before it became a scientific discipline. In fact, we believe that it is pedagogy that can give intellectual, but also practical, consistency to the field of early childhood. Pedagogy, both as a knowledge-tradition dating as far back as to when humans started to think about education of new generations, and as a scientific discipline, is marked by a different logic than that of the individualistic, economic and abstract formalism we encounter today. Pedagogy harbours a logic of *contextuality*, *complexity* and *relationality*. In that sense, pedagogy is in essence a value-driven endeavour, as it is about how early childhood services contribute to democracy, to inclusion, to ethical and esthetical practices, and where democracy or "a good life" cannot be reduced only to intellectual discourse. The confrontation of manifold ideas and practices (and thus the contestation of the dominance of one single discourse) is therefore essential for pedagogy to exist. This is what this groundbreaking series *Contesting Early Childhood* has been doing under the inspired editorial leadership of Peter Moss and Gunilla Dahlberg. And this is what we, as new series editors, wish to continue. And, as this first book is indeed contesting, it is so only in order to open up to other agentic narratives by scholars, policy makers and – most of all – practitioners, student-teachers and lecturers in early childhood teacher education, all essential figures for today and tomorrow's early childhood settings, and capable not only of contesting, but also of *transforming* the field of early childhood.

Reference

Massumi, B. (2002) Parables for the virtual: Movement, affect, sensation. Durham NC.: Duke University Press.

1

INTRODUCTION: CONSTRUCTIONS OF TRUTH IN EARLY CHILDHOOD EDUCATION

A history of the present abuse of neurosciences

Michel Vandenbroeck

This is not about neuroscience. Rather, it is about how neurosciences have been used or misused – often by scholars and policy makers who are not neuroscientists – in the constructions of Truth about the early years. It critically deals with the impact of the discourse, which is inspired by these Truth constructions, on how we think about children; on how we think about the relations between families and the state; and on how we think about the very meaning of education in general and of early childhood education in particular.

I deliberately write Truth with a capital T. In doing so, I wish to highlight that Truth, as I use the concept here, is not an objective fact, but a construction, a way of seeing, and thus – inevitably – a way of not seeing (Burke, 1984). It needs to be clear that the objective of this chapter – and thus of this book – is neither to criticise the claims made by neuroscience, nor to amend the progress that neuroscientists have made in understanding how the brain develops and works, progress that is illustrated by the contribution of Wim Fias further in this book. Neither has this introduction any intentions to criticise the people who call themselves neuroscientists nor the scientific methods they use. Nevertheless, the intention is to offer a critical look at how the neurosciences are popularised for advocacy reasons, and how brain sciences are used to make political claims (about what equal opportunities mean, for instance); or how they are misused, narrowing the meaning of early childhood education (as a machine for early learning, for instance) and parenting (as a series of skills, for instance). This book also aims to offer a critique on how this so-called abuse of neurosciences has influenced our understanding of poverty (as a result of educational poverty and thus intergenerational, rather than as the result of an unequal distribution of material resources and other goods). Or, as Helen Penn argues in her chapter, how it has obscured the discussion on poverty.

I also wish to criticise how the neurosciences are used to shape early childhood education as a commodity and an investment of which we expect an economic return.

And, most of all, it criticises how these Truth claims have become so dominant that it is now difficult to look at children and early years' policies outside of this dominant paradigm. In sum, the aim is to criticise how in a certain socio-political context, a specific form of Truth about early childhood emerges, how the use of science plays a crucial role in such constructions, and how these regimes of Truth – in turn – also shape specific power relations that render children and parents into objects of intervention. As Jan De Vos explains in his chapter, brainification and digitalisation may profoundly change our perceptions on the very essence of education.

Eventually, I also aim to criticise the democratic deficit of such Truth constructions. In that sense, this introductory chapter is a contemporary illustration of the much older knowledge-power paradigm that was studied by Michel Foucault from his early work on dominant discourses (1971) to his later and more subtle work on the construction of the knowledge of the self (Foucault, 1993, 2001a).

A short paradigmatic note

The central Foucauldian question is not "what is power", but rather "where does it come from" and "how does it operate". Power, for Foucault, is less repressive than it is productive (Deleuze, 1985):

> One needs to acknowledge that power relations produce knowledge (and not only because they favour knowledge for its practical use), that power and knowledge are mutually linked, and that there is no power relation without the construction of a field of knowledge, nor is there knowledge that does not suppose and construct power relations (Foucault, 1975, p. 36., translation by Vandenbroeck).[1]

Power produces educational practices by determining how problems are constituted, how people are classified and what are considered appropriate ways to shape behaviour (Moss et al., 2000). Popkewitz (1996) argued therefore that pedagogy is a specific site, which relates political rationalities to the capabilities of the individual. This is very much in line with the view of Paulo Freire (1970, p. 152) who stated: "The parent-child relationship in the home usually reflects the objective cultural conditions of the surrounding social structure." What these authors refer to is that what we believe to be the Truth about early childhood education is always contingent with the wider social and political context. We need to analyse how, historically, early childhood education has been framed as a solution to a socially constructed problem (Vandenbroeck et al., 2010). Visions about what is good for children, what are parental responsibilities, when states need to interfere, and what is the very meaning of early childhood are indeed not a-historical, and neither are the sciences that inform them. As a result, it is important to understand the constructions of neuroscience in early childhood education in their historical dimensions. This calls for a *genealogical* approach, meaning, according to Foucault (2001a, p. 1493):

I start from how a problem is presented in the present and try to make the genealogy of it. So what I try to do is to make the history of relations between thought and truth, a history of thoughts, in the sense that it constitutes a history of truths.[2]

As Escolano (1996) claimed in a seminal paper on a hermeneutical approach of the history of education, this stance asks for an evaluation of the internal coherence of the organisation of data and discourse and their external coherence with the social context and with other concordant or discordant stories. This introductory chapter will very briefly do so for two periods in the history of early childhood education: the early twentieth century and the constructions of prophylaxis and eugenics; and the post–World War II period with the constructions of attachment and developmental psychology, before turning to the present and the constructions of neuroscience. So, once again, when we look at – for instance – the use of prophylactic knowledge gathered by Pasteur, Koch or Lister at the turn of the previous century or the theories of Bowlby and Gesell after World War II, the aim is not to challenge this knowledge or criticise the validity of the claims that were made. Nor do I wish to make a judgement on their intentions. Rather the aim is to contribute to our understanding of how, in a specific socio-political context, these sciences became dominant and how they were shaped and contributed to shaping power relations in the field in the early years. In so doing, I hope to shed some light on change and continuity in the present era of neuroscientific constructions that dominate early childhood discourses.

To warrant, for the country, a strong and beautiful race[3]

The first period we briefly sketch is the beginning of the twentieth century: a period that marked the origins of organised day care in many European countries (Vandenbroeck, 2003). It was a period in which a huge gap between the bourgeoisie and the emerging labour class existed, due to extremely low wages and poor living conditions of the latter (Scholliers, 1995). It was just impossible for a family to feed more than one child with one income and the living conditions of labour families were less than poor, even according to the then-prevailing standards (Lafontaine, 1985). The early twentieth century was also marked by a rather harsh liberal welfare state, since it was consensual – at least among the bourgeoisie, the only citizens who had the right to vote – that the State should not intervene in private matters. As a result, there were no such measures as sickness leave, paid maternity leave, allowances or health insurances. It does not come as a surprise that child mortality was very high: 15 to 25 per cent of children did not live to see their first birthday (Plasky, 1909; Poulain & Tabutin, 1989). Both the living conditions and child mortality were sources of social uproar that challenged the social order and led to the creation of labour class movements in most industrialised cities, and subsequently to the use of strikes as a political weapon. As a result, child mortality was a rising source of concern for the leading class as well. Three scientific disciplines helped to frame this child mortality problem and to construct it as a pedagogical problem that needed intervention: statistics, eugenics and prophylaxis. The statistical sciences were originally considered as an art of governing (Fendler, 2006) and gained scientific status in this period. In the first governmental report on child mortality in Belgium, for instance, many statistical analyses were used to exclude weather conditions as a possible cause for child mortality, as well as other potential causes, and eventually to frame the problem as a problem of labour class neighbourhoods (Velghe, 1919). Inspired by the evolutionary biology of Darwin, social Darwinism (e.g. Spencer) and the neo-Malthusians (Williams, 2000), the eugenic sciences were considered as a leading source of knowledge on the importance of building a strong race for the recent nation states. As an example, the prestigious scientific Solvay Institute established the Belgian Office for Eugenics in Brussels in 1922 (Nationaal Werk voor Kinderwelzijn, 1922). It is probably not a coincidence that the attention for a strong race occurred in a period of industrialisation where health was increasingly perceived as an important economic good (Foucault, 1975). Supported by this eugenic turn, child mortality became a State affair. The premature death of a child was now not only considered as an offence of the mother towards her child, but also as an offence of the mother towards society as a whole. The new prophylactic sciences (e.g. Louis Pasteur in France, Robert Koch in Germany or Joseph Lister in England) had indeed discovered the origins of infectious diseases, as well as ways to prevent them. And with this new knowledge came a large offensive to civilise the labour class and to inform working class mothers about the new prophylactic wisdom, resulting in the mushrooming of charity initiatives such as infant consultation schemes and crèches (Vandenbroeck, 2006). These institutions often also had an implicit aim of soothing the discontent of the labour class. Their civilising function was even quite explicit in Marbeau's much used handbook for the bourgeois charities that wished to initiate child care in France and beyond. In the chapter about the eventual opening of the crèche, Marbeau (1845, p. 91) wrote:

> The poor mothers await this day like the arrival of the Messiah. A touching ceremony will show the indigent that the authority, seconded by the rich, watches over the children with maternal kindness; and the holy bells announce to the poor that one cares for him and to the rich that he has to give (translation by Vandenbroeck).[4]

It is an eloquent example of what Freire (1970, p. 44) wrote on charity:

> Any attempt to "soften" the power of the oppressor in deference to the weakness of the oppressed almost always manifests itself in the form of false generosity; indeed, the attempt never goes beyond this. In order to have the continued opportunity to express their "generosity", the oppressors must perpetuate injustice as well.

In sum, statistics framed the social problem of child mortality as a labour class problem; eugenics legitimated State intervention in a liberal – and thus non-interventionist – welfare state, whilst the prophylaxis explained how the problem needed to be solved. As a result, this scientific Truth contributed to construct the causes of child mortality as either the neglect of culpable mothers, or their ignorance, labelled as "stupid prejudices" of mothers who did "not even read the brochures we distribute to them" (Velghe, 1919). In reality, many of these mothers lacked the means to follow the advice, considering that, for instance, the wood or the coals that were necessary to sterilise the teats were unaffordable for them. The solution of the social problem – which was in the meantime translated into an educational problem – was believed to be provided by philanthropic provision that was based on charity and thus on a moral of the social order, not on civil rights. It is a typical illustration of how a social problem was politically framed as an individual problem and how science was (mis)used to legitimise this individualisation of responsibility.

The steady growth of evidence

Among the most significant developments of psychiatry during the past quarter of a century has been the steady growth of evidence that the quality of the parental care, which a child receives in his earliest years is of vital importance for his future mental health (Bowlby, 1953, p. 13).

This quote from John Bowlby, psychiatrist and "founding father" of attachment theory, is eloquent of the modernist belief in science as progress. After the Second World War, affluent societies were marked by an impressive optimism in the future and an unwavering belief in science as the pathway to welfare and happiness. It was the period in which more democratic – rights-based – welfare states were emerging (including general voting rights, social security, minimal wages, etc.) in most European countries. From the 1950s to the 1970s economies were prosperous, unemployment was historically low and – together with social security and other protective measures – this resulted in a dramatic decrease of poverty and child mortality, at least in affluent European countries. As an example: while child mortality in Belgium was still around 10 per cent shortly after WWII, it was only around 2 per cent in 1968 (Nationaal Werk voor Kinderwelzijn, 1970). This caused serious legitimation problems to the vast *dispositive*[5] of child welfare organisations throughout Europe. It was developmental psychology, starting with attachment theory, that took over the prescribing role of the prophylactic sciences. The World Health Organisation (1946) broadened its definition of health to also include mental and social well-being, and in doing so, it broadened its definition of health as "not merely the absence of infirmity". As a result, the entire population – both healthy and unhealthy – became a potential target for preventive measures. One example of this is the massive introduction of the Apgar score in the 1950s, giving a first assessment report to all new-born children on a 10-point scale. Another salient example is the rapid popularisation of the attachment theory. First developed by John Bowlby on behalf of the WHO, it was soon *naturalised* by Harlow (1958) and his experiments with monkeys and cloth mother surrogates. What Harlow essentially did was to demonstrate that attachment and the basic need of the young child for maternal love were simply natural: an indisputable part of both human and animal nature. In the 1970s Mary Ainsworth (Ainsworth & Bell, 1970) further completed the work and gave it an even more indisputable stance by making attachment measurable, categorisable and thus even more scientifically True. With the Strange Situation test, she developed a diagnostic instrument that aimed at distinguishing the normal from the pathological. The work of Bowlby, Harlow and Ainsworth offer some examples of the rapidly growing discipline of developmental psychology and the proliferation of developmental tests, monitoring and screening methods that contributed to a new understanding of normalcy. In that sense, it can be argued that developmental psychology functioned as what Foucault (1975) described:

> The exercise allows a perpetual characterisation of the individual, either com-pared to the norm, compared to other individuals, or compared to the type of trajectory…
>
> The perpetual penalty running through all points and controlling all moments of the disciplinary institutions compares, differentiates, hierarchises, homogenises and excludes. In sum, it *normalises* (Foucault, 1975, pp. 189, 215. Original emphasis; translation by Vandenbroeck).[6]

Developmental psychology in general and attachment theory in particular have been the subjects of severe criticism since the 1990s, including from feminist theorists (Burman, 1994; Canella, 1997; Singer, 1993). It is indeed probably not a coin-cidence that the earlier versions of attachment theory – urging mothers to take care of their child in the home – gained momentum after the wars, when women were no longer wanted in the industry and it was considered that women better return to their traditional bourgeois roles. Neither is it probably a coincidence that the attention for cognitive development increased in the period of the Cold War. Indeed, after the Sputnik shock (Martens & Niemann, 2010) the West was afraid to lose the race to space and increasingly became aware that nation states could hardly afford themselves not to exploit the full intellectual potential of the population. What is of concern here is how developmental psychology contributed to change the views on children. The metaphor of developmental phases, introducing the image of the child climbing stairs, and the adulto-centric nature of this metaphor originated from this period and were there to stay. According to this new science, each phase in the child's development builds on the former and thus, when something causes concern, the problem needs to be analysed in relation to what went wrong in the previous stage. The succession of developmental stages is perceived, according to this Truth, as a steady evolution towards the better, the stronger and the more intelligent, with the adult as its apogee. Together with this metaphor, measurable norms appeared about what a child should be able to do at what age, accompanied by an implicit understanding that the sooner was also the better in a kind of Olympic Games – citius, altius, fortius – of development. Consequently, this new knowledge led to the discovery of the baby and a renewed focus on the early years, as it is during this period that the foundations of development are built.

The Sputnik shock, as well as the pressure from the civil rights movements, gave rise to new educational programmes in the U.S. (and later in Europe) for what were then called "disadvantaged children" (Beatty, 2012; Beatty & Zigler, 2012). After a first few years of euphoric scientific news, the results became more disappointing as it became clear that the expected benefits did not last much longer than the programmes. In line with the developmental approach, it was argued that this supposed failure was due to the fact that interventions came too late and thus initiated a plea to be more concerned with early education, framing the preschool as a preparation for school. Interestingly, the supposed failure of Head Start projects was, in the early 1970s, also used to legitimate the political decision to shift the attention from the public to the private sphere, and to focus more on interventions in the family (Beatty & Zigler, 2012). Accordingly, there was a growing consensus in the scientific community that a stronger focus on the role of the "disadvantaged" parent was needed. Uri Bronfenbrenner was one of the leading critics of the early compensation programmes and advocated for broadening the programmes and rendering parents into objects of intervention:

> The relations between parents and children should be reinforced … The learning of the child will then be enhanced, and so eventually a more stable interpersonal system will develop, that will be able to foster the development of the child and ensure its future (Bronfenbrenner, 1974, p. 25. Translation by Vandenbroeck).[7]

In sum, after the period in which the problem of child mortality was "solved", developmental psychology gave a new legitimation to the concern for labour class families – or the *Negro Family*, as they were called in the Moynihan report (Beatty & Zigler, 2012). Parents were now supposed to be the lay teachers of their children, which has been labelled as the pedagogicalisation of parents (Popkewitz, 2003) – or even better: mothers. Again, the focus was rather on maternal responsibility than on the shared responsibility between the public and the private domains. Burman (1994) quotes the early work of Gesell (1950) to illustrate this focus on the mother's responsibility: "It is as if the nervous system of the child is completed by the mother. It is her role to think ahead for the child." In the context of the Cold War, the political attention for the educational gap gained momentum. Again, however, the educational gap was not framed as a societal problem of inequality, but rather as a "socio-cultural handicap" of individual families (De Landsheere, 1973). The scientific field shifted its attention from the medical to the psychological. Yet, the use of this scientific field to frame specific families as objects of intervention, without including the families in the debates of what their alleged problem was, did not significantly change.

Third Way politics in times of crisis

The entire period from the late 1970s to the present is marked by consecutive economic crises and rather brief intermediate, slightly more prosperous, intervals. In the late 1970s, the oil crisis caused unemployment, dislocation of industry to low-wage countries and lasting budgetary problems for all affluent nations. This has hardly changed until and beyond the banking crisis at the beginning of the twenty-first century. It is an era marked by globalisation: events that happen thousands of miles away have direct influence on the intimacy of our daily lives. The explosion of the nuclear plant in Chernobyl in 1986 directly affected the food of millions of families in Europe; the developing Chinese economy raised oil prices in Europe; and the irresponsible greed of U.S. and European bankers influenced the home situations of millions of citizens worldwide. It is the era of the "new social question" (Lorenz, 2005): the growing idea that nation states fail in protecting their citizens against unemployment, poverty and other matters. Rosanvallon (1995) argued that the end of the twentieth century was marked by a triple crisis: a financial crisis (states were faced with increased spending in social security issues such as unemployment benefits, while facing reduced income); a bureaucratic crisis (states were increasingly perceived as being ineffective and inefficient by the general population as well as by policy makers); and a philosophical crisis (raising questions about the very concept of social welfare and social security). It is well documented how this crisis gave fertile grounds to what has been labelled as "Third Way politics": alleged consensual policies with a growing focus on risk-management, individual responsibility and a discourse of "no rights without duties" (Vandenbroeck et al., 2010). Different names have been given to the profound changes in the welfare state organisation that these policies engendered, such as the "employment first welfare state" (Finn, 2003) or the "contractual state" (Crawford, 2003). Among the many different aspects of this era, there are three characteristics that I wish to bring to the fore, in order to understand the prevalence of the neuro-arguments in early childhood education in present times: everything must be consensual; everything must be economical; and the layperson cannot see.

Everything must be consensual

Typical for Third Way politics is the search for consensual rather than conflicting policies. The Third Way was developed as the one single possible answer to contemporary societal challenges, and policies had the ambition to overcome the disputes between the political left and the political right (Mouffe, 2005). The slogan that summarises this could be TINA (There Is No Alternative). The core idea of "no rights without duties" and the contingent shift from welfare to justice (Wacquant, 2002) was not only a matter of policy makers, but was in many instances co-constructed by social work itself (Bradt, 2009). This is reflected in the shift of policies from combating poverty to combating child poverty. As analysed by Morabito et al. (2013), a shift occurred from redistributive policies (e.g. through taxation, social welfare) aiming at equality of outcomes to policies aiming at equality of opportunities. The World Bank advocated this as a consensual policy:

> The idea of giving people equal opportunity early in life, whatever their socioeconomic background, is embraced across the political spectrum – as a matter of fairness for the left and as a matter of personal effort for the right. ... Thus, shifting the debate from inequality of income or earnings to inequality of opportunity, and to the policies needed to tackle that inequality, might facilitate a political and policy consensus. When the focus of the debate is on inequality of income or any other outcome, the views about how much to redistribute – if any at all – and through which mechanisms would vary from left to right across the political spectrum. However, when the focus shifts to the equalization of opportunity, political consensus about the need to reduce inequity is easier to achieve, and the direction this principle gives to policy is clearer (Paes de Barros *et al.*, 2009, pp. xvii; 27).

As a result, early childhood education comes into the picture as the potential and consensual solution to many social problems. Indeed, while state intervention in the redistribution of outcomes is increasingly considered as problematic, interventions in early childhood education cannot be suspected of benefiting the "undeserving poor". No one can blame the child for being poor, can one? Early years investments are promoted as being the greatest potential equaliser, by both international organisations such as UNESCO (see Morabito *et al.*, 2013 for some examples), and policy makers. In his report on combating poverty to the British government, Frank Field (2010, p. 5) wrote:

> It is family background, parental education, good parenting and the opportunities for learning and development in those crucial years that together matter more to children than money, in determining whether their potential is realised in adult life.

There is a remarkable resemblance to be noticed with a nineteenth-century handbook for bourgeois charity stating: "of all causes of indigence, education is the most important" (de Gérandot, 1820, p. 12., translation by Vandenbroeck).[8]

Everything must be economic

Despite the fact that nation states have less impact on their national economies in the global market – or maybe because of that – all policies have a particular focus on economic aspects. This also affects what previously was called the "non-profit sector" and renamed itself after the first economic crisis as the "social profit sector", thus adopting an economic discourse and contributing to the marketisation of the social. The dominance of economic issues obviously also affected early childhood education. First, this was noticeable by an increasing commodification and marketisation of early childhood education, based on the assumptions that markets enhance competition and thus warrant quality and economic efficiency (for a thorough critique of these assumptions, see Lloyd & Penn, 2013; Moss, 2009). Second, the commodification is also noticeable in the ways in which early childhood policies are increasingly discussed with economic arguments, including the famous "return on investment" argument (e.g. Barnett & Masse, 2007). It is hard, nowadays, to find a policy document on early childhood education that does not quote Nobel Prize laureate James Heckman, often also including his famous "Heckman curve", illustrating that investing in the youngest children yields the highest economic returns (Heckman, 2006). There seems to be little criticism about the very idea that social and educational policies are primarily justified in pragmatic economic terms and that democratic and value-based arguments seem to have disappeared from the public debate (Moss, 2007; Mouffe, 2005).

The layperson cannot see

Immediately after the nuclear disaster in Chernobyl, Ulrich Beck (1987) wrote an interesting essay on the "anthropological shock" this caused. He explained that the urgent warning the next day, that one should not let one's children play in the sandbox, was followed by the unverifiable denial that this recommendation had any validity whatsoever. What Chernobyl did to society, Beck explained, was that danger and its consequences became invisible. While experts contradicted each other on television, this "deprivation of our senses" provoked the paradoxical reaction that laypersons became even more attracted to and dependent on the experts (Beck, 1987). Rose and Abi-Rached made a very similar claim when it comes to the "imaging business" of neurosciences:

> We, the laypersons cannot see. We need the designation of those who have the authority to see, including the imagers. ... To render visible, that is to say, requires conditions of possibility within a larger, networked, distributed, assembled field of intensities and powers – connecting up such diverse sites as the clinic, the lab, the pharmaceutical company, popular literature, and the mass media. ... The image, despite suggestions to the contrary, and despite all the arguments black-boxed within it, does not speak for itself – it has to be spoken for (Rose & Abi-Rached, 2013, pp. 55–56).

This brings us to the core of the argument: the current status of the neurosciences and their (mis)use in social and educational policies.

The progressives' faith in technical expertise for solving social problems[9]

> The foundations of brain architecture are established early in life through a continuous series of dynamic interactions in which environmental conditions and personal experiences have a significant impact on how genetic predispositions are expressed (National Scientific Council on the Developing Child, 2007, p. 1).

Since the turn of the millennium the neuro-argument about early childhood education is prevailing, raising the expectation that the neurosciences will explain it all (De Vos & Pluth, 2016). Neurosciences and brain images are increasingly popping up in documents of policy makers, but also of NGOs, advocating for investments in the early years. A typical example is the report on early intervention by MP Graham Allen to the British government (Allen, 2011). The Allen Report showed the much-abused image of a shrunken "nutshell" brain on its cover, insinuating that a lack of care in the early years would cause such a deteriorated brain.[10] The report argues that considering the rapid growth of the brain in the first two years, we can realise

> reaping massive savings in public expenditure for the smallest of investments in better outcomes, and by avoiding expensive provision when things go wrong (Allen, 2011, p. vii).

A few years later, in a paper advocating "Social Impact Bonds" (Allen, s.d.), he argued that early years interventions are too challenging for the public sector, yet – considering that long term returns on investment are proven – they should be privately financed and this would promote competition and thus drive innovation. Another example is the report that MPs from different parties wrote, urging the British government to invest both in antenatal classes and in "evidence-based services" for "at-risk families" in the first "critical 1001 days" as that restricted period is believed to be a key moment for brain development, because:

> We know too that not intervening now will affect not just this generation of children and young people but also the next (Leadsom et al., 2010, p. 2).

The use of this nexus of brain research and economic arguments is not just the privilege of policy makers. It is also used by NGOs. An example is the brochure with the title "Lighting up your brains", published by Save the Children. The brochure argues that brain research has shown that parents need to enhance the "Home Learning Environment" (and it spells out what behaviour parents need to deploy "to help build your child's brain"), next to a plea for high quality nurseries (Finnegan & Lawton, 2016). The document frequently uses terms such as "wired in the brain", "brain architecture", "sensitive" or "critical periods" and "toxic stress", and we can increasingly find these terms in publications from international NGOs (e.g. Marope & Kaga, 2015).

That is, of course, no coincidence. Scholars from the National Scientific Council on the Developing Child (Harvard University) joined forces in a seven-year project with communication specialists (FrameWorks Institute) to "frame" brain research in such ways that it would better influence policy makers and other laypeople. Using different panels and interviews with laypeople to examine which concepts would have the most impact, the communication specialists came up with the following metaphors (or "frame elements"): "brain architecture", "toxic stress", "serve and return" and the image of the "circuitry" of the brain as best options for a "simplifying model" that could enhance policy impact (Shonkoff & Bales, 2011). The communication effort was the logical pursuit of a group of scholars who claimed that it was time for a "more robust Science-to-Policy Agenda" (Shonkoff & Leavitt, 2010, p. 690).

> The contribution of neuroscience to innovation in social policy could be formidable. Basic and clinical research over the past two decades have created a highly promising yet underdeveloped interface between these two worlds [neuroscience and social policy] that would benefit considerably from a more permeable boundary (Shonkoff & Leavitt, 2010, p. 691).

High-level scholarly journals in this field (e.g. *Science*) argued that policy makers "should champion the adoption and sustenance of legislation consistent with the findings of that research. They should translate good science into good public policy" (Gormley, 2011, p. 978). The article suggested that scholars should publish short texts (the average length of a successful policy brief in the U.S. Congress being 2.91 pages) that describe consensus, since "research is less likely to be used, when there is no scholarly consensus" (Gormley, 2011, p. 979). What this may mean in practice is illustrated by a much cited brochure from the National Scientific Council on the Developing Child (2007, pp. 6–7):

> The basic principles of neuroscience indicate the need for a far greater sense of urgency regarding the prompt resolution of such decisions as when to remove a child from the home, when and where to place a child in foster care, when to terminate parental rights, and when to move towards a permanent placement. The window of opportunity for remediation in a child's developing brain architecture is time-sensitive and time-limited.

The citation above makes perfectly clear how this form of Truth construction inevitably leads to the objectification of children and parents, an objectification that erases all space for dialogue. It reduces policy to the application of "scientific" advice, rather than as the organisation of antagonistic debate (Mouffe, 2005). When science produces indisputable Truth and policies are reduced to its application, this presents the end of what Mouffe calls "the political".

This one-sided use of developmental neuroscience and the accompanying simplified concepts have received much criticism from within the neurosciences. Much of this criticism is about the concept of critical periods that does not sufficiently take into account the plasticity of the brain (Blakemore & Frith, 2005; Bruer, 2011; Maguire *et al.*, 2000; H. Rose & Rose, 2012). In addition, there have been serious methodological warnings about oversimplifications and even suspicious interpretations of results of fMRI and other visualisations of brain activity (Bennett *et al.*, 2009; Bettis, 2012; Vul *et al.*, 2009). Even though the neurosciences have indeed made great progress in understanding the relations between economic adversity and brain development (Neville *et al.*, 2013; Noble *et al.*, 2015), the claim made by Bruer in 1997 that basing social policy on neuroscience is "a bridge too far", however, still holds today (Bruer, 1997).

Discussion

The constructions of neuroscience in early childhood education show some continuity with previous regimes of Truth in this field. Yet, considering the many ethical issues, as well as the methodological flaws, one could wonder why policy makers from both the left and the right – together with advocacy NGOs – are lured by the sirens of neuroscience. One possible explanation is of course the alleged consensus on the shift from redistributive social policies to equality of opportunities, as described above. Another important aspect is that the use of brain images adds to the credibility of the message. Legrenzi and Umiltà, two renowned neuroscientists who often stood up against the misuse of neuroscientific arguments, narrate an interesting experiment conducted at Yale University showing that psychology students more readily judged a message as true when it was accompanied by images of brain scans, even when these had nothing to do with the content of the message (Legrenzi & Umiltà, 2011). This may be attractive for frustrated activists who since several decades advocated – often in vain – for more attention for the early years, especially when faced with austerity policies that threaten to reduce the budgets for social and educational matters. It may indeed appear tempting to early years activists to argue that the investments in the early years pay off, and in so doing one can then justify one's profession. However, by using the neuro-economic argument of the return on investments, they inevitably reinforce the idea that the only argument that matters is indeed economic.

A most important aspect of the seductive characteristics of the brain argument is the historical continuity in viewing children as the object of policy – saving the world, one child at the time. Inevitably, the image of the fragile child as a future of the nation, and the salvation narratives that go with it, frame parents as suspicious (Hendrick, 1997). The focus on deficit parents has even increased with the use of neuroscientific Truth, which is reflected in the proliferation of parent training programmes and their discourse on parenting skills (Macvarish *et al.*, 2015). It is probably not a coincidence that in times when man-made risks become uncontrollable – be it ecological or economical – the mirage of the feasible child becomes even more attractive. As Furedi (2014, pp. ix–x) argued:

> When leading politicians on both sides of the Atlantic can argue that bad parenting harms more children than poverty, then it becomes evident that parental determinism has become the mirror image of economic determinism.

This seems to be precisely what is at stake here: a neurobiological-economic nexus in which childhood is merely the preamble of adult productivity in a meritocratic society. Scholars of that nexus indeed warn us that:

A growing proportion of the U.S. workforce will have been raised in dis-advantaged environments that are associated with relatively high proportions of individuals with diminished cognitive and social skills. A cross-disciplinary examination of research in economics, developmental psychology, and neu-robiology reveals a striking convergence on a set of common principles that account for the potent effects of early environment on the capacity for human skill development (Knudsen *et al.*, 2006, p. 10155).

What we learn from this history of the present is that what is considered as True is not a-historical and what is considered as valuable and valid Science is always related to the socio-political context. The context today is one in which the welfare state is much less considered as the necessary compensation for inevitable unfair effects of the free market, but rather as one of global capitalism in which welfare expenditures are constructed as avoidable inefficient threats to the free market. This has profound effects on the discussion on the very significance of education and pedagogy. While the meaning of education is narrowed down to issues of pro-ductivity, early childhood education risks being reduced to early learning. Early learning in itself, then, becomes a mere preparation for the real learning that takes place in compulsory school (Moss, 2013). In the same vein, pedagogy risks being reduced to the development of effective methods to achieve the predefined goals. And social pedagogy then is nothing more than an attempt to keep some attention for the relational – some would say holistic – aspects of this utilitarian pedagogy. In sum, pedagogy – including social pedagogy – is then reduced to the search for doing things right, while leaving out the question of what is the right thing to do.

When education is instrumentalised as the road towards a predefined goal that lies beyond childhood, this inevitably raises the question about who is entitled to define this goal. Who can participate in the debate about what early childhood education is for? And this is where the bio-economic nexus leaves no space for debate. It is the democratic deficit of "There Is No Alternative". This means that parents are reduced to "beings for others" in the Freirian sense. According to Freire (1970, p. 60) science and technology can be used to reduce men to the status of "things"; yet they can also be used to promote humanisation, since the essence of education as problem posing education responds to the essence of consciousness, rejects communiqués and embodies communication.

The debate continues

In the next chapters, scholars from diverse disciplines have been invited to react to this introduction. First, Jan De Vos, a critical philosopher, criticises the distinction that was made between neuroscience and the use of neuroscience. He takes the analysis a decisive step further by reflecting on how neurologisation and digitalisation affect how we construct the subject, or better still, how it constructs and deconstructs the (minimal) subject and thus our image of the child and of education itself, as an act of separation between the public and the private. Sue White and Dave Wastell continue by more thoroughly uncovering the misuse of neuroscience in two major and influential U.K. documents: the Allen Report, mentioned in the introduction, and "A Child's Timeframe", a report on the removal of infants from their families based on the *precautionary principle*. In so doing, they develop further one of the arguments in this introduction on the entanglement of policy and science, claiming that the imperative of policy is to persuade, not to faithfully present the state of the scientific field.

Helen Penn then elaborates on an aspect that has only been developed in this introductory chapter in more shallow ways: how the use of the neurosciences has contributed to avoid the discussion on poverty. This may very well be one of the reasons why the neurodiscourse became so popular. Helen Penn opens up our perspective beyond the Eurocentric lens and brings in elements of how brain sciences have been used to support programmes and assumptions in developing countries, in the context of global neoliberalism.

Finally, Wim Fias, a neuroscientist, criticises how from the onset we simplistically may view the neurosciences as a homogeneous area. Through a concrete case study on the study of the neural basis for mathematical cognition, he gives an insight in how the neurosciences, being a very young science, develop. And in so doing, he allows us a view from the inside on the progress of this science, but also on how distorted images of alleged findings get popularised.

Notes

1 Il faut plutôt admettre que le pouvoir produit du savoir [...], pouvoir et savoir s'impliquent directement l'un l'autre; qu'il n'y a pas de relation de pouvoir sans constitution corrélative d'un champ de savoir, ni de savoir qui ne suppose et ne constitue en même temps des relations de pouvoir. [...] Mais il ne faut pas s'y tromper: on n'a pas substitué à l'âme, illusion des théologiens, un homme réel, objet de savoir, de réflexion philosophique ou d'intervention technique. L'homme dont on nous parle et qu'on invite à libérer est déjà en lui-même l'effet d'un assujettissement bien plus profond que lui. [...] Cette âme [...] est l'élément où s'articulent les effets d'un certain type de pouvoir et la référence d'un savoir, l'engrenage par lequel les relations de pouvoir donnent lieu à un savoir possible, et le savoir reconduit et renforce les effets du pouvoir.

2 Je pars d'un problème dans les termes où il se pose actuellement et j'essaie d'en faire la généalogie. Généalogie veut dire que je mène l'analyse à partir d'une question présente. [...] Ce que j'essaie de faire, c'est l'histoire des rapports que la pensée entretient avec la vérité; l'histoire de la pensée en tant qu'elle est pensée de la vérité.

3 From a speech by Elise Plasky on 5 February, 1910 in which she tried to convince decision makers to build more crèches (Plasky, 1910).

4 Les pauvres mères attendent ce jour comme le Messie. Une cérémonie touchante fait voir aux indigents que l'autorité, secondée par les riches, veille sur leurs enfants avec une sollicitude maternelle, et la cloche sainte annonce au pauvre qu'on pense à lui, annonce au riche qu'il faut donner.

5 Foucault uses the term *dispositif* to designate a heterogeneous assemblage of discourses, institutional regulations, scientific statements, political propositions, even architectural designs, etc. that are not necessarily contingent, but that together have a strategically dominating function (which is not the same as saying that they have a dominating goal or are purposefully designed as an assemblage) (Foucault, 2001b, pp. 298–299).

6 L'exercice permet une perpétuelle caractérisation de l'individu soit par rapport à ce terme, soit par rapport aux autres individus, soit par rapport à un type de parcours. La pénalité perpétuelle qui traverse tous les points, et contrôle tous les instants des institutions disciplinaires compare, différencie, hiérarchise, homogénéise, exclut. En un mot elle *normalise*.

7 [...] daß sich die Bindungen zwischen den Eltern und dem Kind verstärken [...] daß zich dadurch das lernen des Kindes gefördert wird, und daß schließlich ein stabiles interpersonales Systeem entsteht, das imstande ist, die Entwicklung des Kindes zu fördern und für die Zukunft zu sichern.

8 De toutes les causes de l'indigence, c'est l'éducation la plus importante.

9 It is a quote from William T. Gormley in *Science*, arguing – without any ironic twist – that (neuro)scientists should be more proactive in influencing policy makers (Gormley, 2011, p. 978).

10 See chapter 3 for Sue White and Dave Wastell critique on the unscientific use of this image. See also Williams (2014).

References

Ainsworth, M. D., & Bell, S. M. (1970). Attachment, exploration, and separation: Illustrated by the behavior of one-year-olds in a strange situation. *Child Development*, 41(1), 49–67.

Allen, Graham (2011). Early intervention: Smart investment, massive savings. The second independent report to Her Majesty's Government. London: HM Government.

Allen, Graham (s.d.). *Financing early intervention*. London: http://www.gov.uk.

Barnett, W. S., & Masse, L. N. (2007). Comparative benefit-cost analysis of the Abecedarian program and its policy implications. *Economics of Education Review*, 26(1), 113–125.

Beatty, B. (2012). The debate over the young "disadvantaged child": Preschool intervention, developmental psychology, and compensatory education in the 1960s and early 1970s. *Teachers College Record*, 114(6), 1–36.

Beatty, B., & Zigler, E. (2012). Reliving the history of compensatory education: Policy choices, bureaucracy, and the politicized role of science in the evolution of head start. *Teachers College Record*, 114(6), 1–10.

Beck, U. (1987). The anthropological shock: Chernobyl and the contours of the risk society. *Berkeley Journal of Sociology*, 32, 153–165.

Bennett, C. M., Baird, A. A., Miller, M. B., & Wolford, G. L. (2009). Neural correlates of interspecies perspective taking in a post-mortem Atlantic salmon: An argument for multiple comparisons correction. *Journal of Serendipitous and Unexpected Results*, 1(1), 1–15.

Bettis, R. A. (2012). The search for asterisks: Compromised statistical tests and flawed theories. *Strategic Management Journal*, 33(1), 103–113.

Blakemore, S. J., & Frith, U. (2005). The learning brain: Lessons for education: A précis. *Developmental Science*, 8(6), 459–471.

Bowlby, J. (1953). *Child care and the growth of love*. London: Pelican Books.

Bradt, L. (2009). Social work and the shift from "welfare" to "justice". *British Journal of Social Work*, 39(1), 113–127.

Bronfenbrenner, U. (1974). *Wie wirksam ist kompensatorische Erziehung?* Stuttgart, Germany: Erst Klett Verlag.

Bruer, J. T. (1997). Education and the brain: A bridge too far. *Educational Researcher*, 26(8), 4–16.

Bruer, J. T. (2011). *Revisiting "The myth of the first three years"*. Canterbury, UK: Centre for Parenting Culture Studies, Kent University.

Burke, K. (1984). *Permanence and change: In retrospective prospect*. Berkeley, CA: University of California Press.

Burman, E. (1994). *Deconstructing developmental psychology*. London: Routledge.

Canella, G. (1997). *Deconstructing early childhood education: social justice and revolution*. New York: Peter Lang.

Crawford, A. (2003). Contractual governance of deviant behaviour. *Journal of Law and Society*, 30(4), 479–505.

de Gérandot, J.-M. (1820). *Le visiteur du pauvre*. Paris: Louis Collas Imprimeur-Editeur.

De Landsheere, G. (1973). *Recherche sur les handicaps socio-culturels de 0 à 7–8 ans*. Bruxelles: Ministère de l'Education nationale et de la Culture Française.

De Vos, J., & Pluth, E. (2016). Introduction. In J. De Vos & E. Pluth (Eds.), *Neuroscience and critique: Exploring the limits of the neurological turn* (pp. 1–8). London: Routledge.

Deleuze, G. (1985). *Foucault*. Paris: Les Editions de Minuit.

Escolano, A. (1996). Postmodernity or high modernity? Emerging approaches in the new history of education. *Paedagogica Historica. International Journal of the History of Education*, 32(2), 325–341.

Fendler, L. (2006). Why generalisability is not generalisable. *Journal of Philosophy of Education*, 40(4), 437–449.

Field, F. (2010). *The foundation years: Preventing poor children becoming poor adults. The report of the independent review on poverty and life chances*. London: HM Government.

Finn, D. (2003). The employment first welfare state: Lessons from the New Deal for young people. *Social Policy and Administration*, 37(7), 709–724.

Finnegan, J., & Lawton, K. (2016). Lighting up young brains. How parents, carers and nurseries support children's brain development in the first five years. Retrieved from http://www.savethechildren.org.uk/sites/default/files/images/Lighting_Up_Young_ Brains1_0CSCupdate.pdf.

Foucault, M. (1971). *L'Ordre du discours*. Paris: Gallimard.

Foucault, M. (1975). *Surveiller et punir*. Paris: Gallimard.

Foucault, M. (1993). About the beginnings of the hermeneutics of the self. *Political Theory*, 21(2), 198–227.

Foucault, M. (2001a). Interview de Michel Foucault. In M. Foucault (Ed.), *Dits et écrits II, 1976–1988* (pp. 1475–1497). Paris: Gallimard.

Foucault, M. (2001b). Le jeu de Michel Foucault. Entretien avec D. Colas *et al.* In M. Foucault (Ed.), *Dits et écrits II, 1976–1988* (pp. 298–329). Paris: Gallimard.

Freire, P. (1970). *Pedagogy of the oppressed*. New York: Herder and Herder.

Furedi, F. (2014). Foreword. In E. Lee, J. Bristow, C. Faircloth & J. Macvarish (Eds.), *Parenting culture studies* (pp. viii–x). London: Palgrave Macmillan.

Gesell, A. (1950). *The first five years of life: A guide to the study of the preschool child*. London: Methuen.

Gormley, W. T. (2011). From science to policy in early childhood education. *Science*, 333(6045), 978–981.

Harlow, H. F. (1958). The nature of love. *American Psychologist*, 13, 673–685.

Heckman, J. J. (2006). Skill formation and the economics of investing in disadvantaged children. *Science*, 312(5782), 1900–1902.

Hendrick, H. (1997). Constructions and reconstructions of British childhood: An interpretative survey, 1800 to present. In A. James & A. Prout (Eds.), *Constructing and reconstructing childhood* (pp. 34–62). London: Falmer Press.

Knudsen, E. I., Heckman, J. J., Cameron, J. L., & Shonkoff, J. P. (2006). Economic, neuro-biological, and behavioral perspectives on building America's future workforce. Retrieved 24 December, 2013 from http://www.pnas.org/content/103/27/10155.full.pdf.

Lafontaine, D. (1985). *Maternité et petite enfance dans le bassin industriel liégois de 1830 à 1940*. Liège: Laboratoire de pédagogie expérimental.

Leadsom, A., Field, F., Burstow, P., & Lucas, C. (2010). *The 1001 critical days: The importance of the conception to age two period*. London: Wave Trust – NSPCC.

Legrenzi, P., & Umiltà, C. (2011). *Neuromania: On the limits of brain science*. New York: Oxford University Press.

Lloyd, H., & Penn, H. (2013). *Childcare markets: Can they deliver an equitable service?* Bristol, UK: The Policy Press.

Lorenz, W. (2005). Social work and a new social order – Challenging neo-liberalism's erosion of solidarity. *Social Work & Society*, 3(1), 93–101.

Macvarish, J., Lee, E., & Lowe, P. (2015). Neuroscience and family policy: What becomes of the parent? *Critical Social Policy*, 35(2), 248–269.

Maguire, E. A., Gadian, D. G., Johnsrude, I. S., Good, C. D., Ashburner, J., Frackowiak, R. S., & Frith, C. D. (2000). Navigation-related structural change in the hippocampi of taxi drivers. *Proceedings of the National Academy of Science*, 97(8), 84398–84403.

Marbeau, J. B. F. (1845). *Des crèches. Ou moyen de diminuer la misère en augmentant la population*. Paris: Comptoir des Imprimeurs-Unis.

Marope, M., & Kaga, Y. (2015). Repositioning ECCE in the post-2015 agenda. In M. Marope & Y. Kaga (Eds.), *Investing against evidence: The global state of early childhood care and education* (pp. 9–33). Paris: UNESCO.

Martens, K., & Niemann, D. (2010). *Governance by comparison. How ratings and rankings impact national policy-making in education* (Vol. 139). Bremen: Universität Bremen.

Morabito, C., Vandenbroeck, M., & Roose, R. (2013). "The greatest of equalisers": A critical review of international organisations' views on early childhood care and education. *Journal of Social Policy*, 42(3), 451–467.

Moss, P. (2007). Bringing politics into the nursery: Early childhood education as a democratic practice. *European Early Childhood Education Research Journal*, 15(1), 5–20.

Moss, P. (2009). *There are alternatives: Markets and democratic experimentalism in early childhood education and care* (Vol. 53). The Hague: Bernard Van Leer Foundation.

Moss, P. (2013). The relationship between early childhood and compulsory education: A properly political question. In P. Moss (Ed.), *Early childhood and compulsory education: Reconceptualising the relationship*. London: Routledge.

Moss, P., Dillon, J., & Statham, J. (2000). The "child in need" and the "rich child": Discourses, constructions and practice. *Critical Social Policy*, 63(2), 233–254.

Mouffe, C. (2005). *On the political*. London: Routledge.

Nationaal Werk voor Kinderwelzijn (1922). Actueele vragen. *Maandblad, October*(1), 1.

Nationaal Werk voor Kinderwelzijn (1970). *Activiteitenverslag voor het jaar 1969*. Brussels: Nationaal Werk voor Kinderwelzijn.

National Scientific Council on the Developing Child (2007). *The timing and quality of early experiences combine to shape brain architecture*. Cambridge, MA: Center on the Developing Child at Harvard University.

Neville, H., Stevens, C., Pakulak, E., & Bell, T. A. (2013). Commentary: Neurocognitive consequences of socioeconomic disparities. *Developmental Science*, 16(5), 708–712.

Noble, K. G., Houston, S. M., Brito, N. H., Bartsch, H., Kan, E., Kuperman, J. M. … Sowell, E. R. (2015). Family income, parental education and brain structure in children and adolescents. *Nature Neuroscience*, 18(5), 773–780.

Paes de Barros, R., Ferreira, F., Molinas Vega, J., & Saavedra Chanduvi, J. (2009). *Measuring inequality of opportunities in Latin America and the Caribbean*. Washington DC: World Bank.

Plasky, E. (1909). *La protection et l'éducation de l'enfant du peuple en Belgique. I. Pour les tout-petits*. Bruxelles: Société belge de libraires.

Plasky, E. (1910). *La crèche et sa nécessité sociale. Conférence donné le 5 février 1910 à l'Exposition d'Hygiène des enfants du premier âge*. Anvers: Buschman.

Popkewitz, T. (1996). Rethinking decentralization and the state/civil society distinctions: The state as problematic governing. *Journal of Educational Policy*, 11(1), 27–51.

Popkewitz, T. (2003). Governing the child and pedagogicalization of the parent: A historical excursus into the present. In M. Bloch, K. Holmlund, L. Moqvist & T. Popkewitz (Eds.), *Governing children, families and education: Restructuring the welfare state* (pp. 35–62). New York: Palgrave.

Poulain, M., & Tabutin, D. (1989). La surmortalité des petites filles. In L. Courtois, J. Pirotte & F. Rosart (Eds.), *Femmes des années 80. Un sciècle de condition feminine en Belgique. 1889–1989.* (pp. 25–31). Louvain-la-Neuve: Academia.

Rosanvallon, P. (1995). *La nouvelle question sociale: Repenser l'Etat-providence.* Paris: Seuil.

Rose, H., & Rose, S. (2012). *Genes, cells and brains: The Promethean promises of the new biology.* London: Verso.

Rose, N., & Abi-Rached, M. (2013). *Neuro: The new brain sciences and the management of the mind.* Princeton, NJ: Princeton University Press.

Scholliers, P. (1995). *A century of real industrial wages in Belgium, 1840–1939.* In P. Scholliers & V. Zamagni (Eds.), *Labour reward: Real wages and economic change in 19th and 20th century Europe* (pp. 106–137). Aldershot: Edward Elgar.

Shonkoff, J. P., & Bales, S. N. (2011). Science does not speak for itself: Translating child development research for the public and its policymakers. *Child Development,* 82(1), 17–32.

Shonkoff, J. P., & Leavitt, P. (2010). Neuroscience and the future of early childhood policy: Moving from why to what and how. *Neuron,* 67(5), 689–691.

Singer, E. (1993). Shared care for children. *Theory and Psychology,* 3(4), 429–449.

Vandenbroeck, M. (2003). From crèches to childcare: Constructions of motherhood and inclusion/exclusion in the history of Belgian infant care. *Contemporary Issues in Early Childhood,* 4(3), 137–148.

Vandenbroeck, M. (2006). The persistent gap between education and care: A "history of the present" research on Belgian child care provision and policy. *Paedagogica Historica. International Journal of the History of Education,* 42(3), 363–383.

Vandenbroeck, M., Coussée, F., & Bradt, L. (2010). The social and political construction of early childhood education. *British Journal of Educational Studies,* 58(2), 139–153.

Velghe, H. (1919). *La protection de l'enfance en Belgique. Son passé, son avenir.* Bruxelles: Goemaere.

Vul, E., Haris, C., Winkielman, P., & Pashler, H. (2009). Puzzling high correlations in fMRI studies of emotion, personality and social cognition. *Perspectives on Psychological Science,* 4(3), 274–290.

Wacquant, L. (2002). *Punir les pauvres. Le nouveau gouvernement de l'insécurité sociale.* Marseille: Agone.

Williams, R. (2000). Social Darwinism. In J. Offer (Ed.), *Herbert Spencer: Critical assessment* (pp. 186–199). London: Routledge.

Williams, Z. (2014). Is misused neuroscience defining early years and child protection policy? *The Guardian,* 26 April. https://www.theguardian.com/education/2014/apr/26/misused-neuroscience-defining-child-protection-policy.

World Health Organisation (1946). *Constitution of the World Health Organisation.* New York: WHO.

2

THE NEUROTURN IN EDUCATION

Between the Scylla of psychologization and the Charybdis of digitalization?

Jan De Vos

Introduction: Ceci n'est pas un pipe.

What if we read the opening phrase of this book "this is not about neuroscience" (see chapter 1) along the famous line of René Margritte, "ceci n'est pas un pipe" ("this is not a pipe")? After all, it is written by a fellow Belgian, so a bit of surrealist phrasing might be involved here. "This is not about neuroscience" meaning, then, while it is not about neuroscience, eventually, in a twisted way it might be about neuroscience after all. That is, engaging with the uses and often pernicious popularizations of neuroscience in education and parenting might reveal some interesting things about proper and academic neuroscience itself.

For, arguably, vis-à-vis much applied and popular neuroscience, the claims of neuroscientists themselves are nuanced and approach human and social reality in a far more careful and tentative way. But perhaps it is expedient to ask why neuroscience, in the first place, needs to be careful and nuanced? Why can't neuroscience simply proceed, slowly but firmly, to plain and unbashful certainty? We must resist the temptation to attribute this solely to the fact that neuroscience is still a young science having a lot to research and to analyse. Nor should we be content with the argument that the brain is such a complex organ (still?) outrunning the intellectual capacity it generates. And, in the same vein, we should not simply resort to the traditional truism of science proceeding by way of provisional and unsettled results. Perhaps, in contrast, the simple but radical point to make is that the indefiniteness and provisionality of the neurosciences is not accidental nor temporal but structural, leading academic neuroscience to caution and nuances, and popular neuroscience to dash forward. Thus the bravados of popular neurosciences might reveal something essential of the neurosciences as such: perhaps the latter cannot claim full closure.

Hence, a critical approach does not stop short of looking at the subsequent uses and abuses of neuroscience; it also engages in a primordial critique of the neurosciences themselves. Critique is here understood in the philosophical tradition of examining the conditions of (im)possibility of science. And perhaps the *via regia* here is precisely to look at what happens with neuroscience leaving the labs: for, is it not clear that when Vandenbroeck looks at how neuroscience leads to con- structions of Truth (how we think about children and what we think education is or should be), then, as he surely would agree, these Truth constructions always already inform and influence basic neuroscience as such? However, perhaps we should not look for the origin of the Truth constructions in the extra-academic interfering with the academic (this could be eliminated or dealt with), but, rather, we should look for their origin within academic rationality itself. Put differently, perhaps the Truth constructions informing and influencing basic neuroscience stem from the sciences as such. And, to cut a long story short, here it is particularly expedient to trace how the old psychological theories, allegedly overcome by the neuro-paradigms, still silently and unwittingly inform and underpin the neu- rosciences (De Vos, 2016b). Is this moreover not the ultimate source of the structural indefiniteness and provisionality of neuroscience? For, eventually, even basic neu- roscientific research is about establishing connections between, on the one hand, neural matter, neural organization or neural activity, and on the other, the human factor. Here, I claim, the psychological theories come back in, to cater for the human factor to be correlated to the neural. Hence, the idea that neuroscience delivers the foundations of psychology is all too simple, in the first instance it is the other way around. Here of course things become complicated: for, if one wants to do neuroscientific research on, for example, empathy, the issue is not only which of the different and often contradictory psychological theories on empathy should be used, but are concepts such as "empathy" not in the first instance historical and social constructs rather than referring to objective and natural categories? Thus, the uses and abuses of neuroscience overstretching or misinterpreting neuroscientific findings might only show in a magnified way that genuine neuroscience itself is always already involved in relying on an interpretational and always questionable jump to make sense of the neurological. As the hidden fundament of the neu- rosciences is the shaky ground of psychology, psychology's argument that it is brain based and neurologically double-checked brings to mind the Von Munchausen- paradox: he who saved himself from drowning by pulling himself out of the swamp by his own hair.

But to make sure, the fact that it is about intra-academic dynamics does not mean that there is no socio-political dimension involved: precisely the postulation of both the psy sciences and neurosciences to be unproblematic objective scientific endeavours preceding the uses and abuses, could be considered as *ideology at its purest*. Of course, here I am extending Slavoj Žižek's argument that today's post-political claim to be beyond ideology (understanding liberal capitalism as the natural system most appropriate for human organization) is the ideological move par excellence (Žižek, 2010, p. 42). Can we not discern an echo of this in the presumption that neuroscience is merely establishing objectively the *natural and material* basis of human and social behaviour? One could argue, this is where neuroscience is particularly ideological and political. Consider again the issue of empathy (currently often researched in relation to the so-called mirror neurons. For a concise critique see Lesnik-Oberstein, 2015). How empathy is conceived – and already the mere fact of calling into life such a concept – entails a particular, non-neutral *political* conceptualization of the human and the social. At the least the ultimately *intra-individual* concept of empathy risks to decontextualize the socio-economical and the political, occluding issues such as inequality and power relations. Hence, most importantly, the ideological dimension of neuroscience perspires in its silent and often occluded recourse to psychology. That is, the typical correlational paradigm driving the neurosciences is where, together with the old psychologies, Trojan horse-like, all kinds of political and ideological images of the human and of society come in.[1]

Hence, instead of elevating the good (enough) neuroscientist to the patron of Innocent Science, we should point to the messiness of the neuroscientific endeavour and hold neuroscientists responsible for it: in the end they make the ideological choices which psychologies are put into. To be absolute clear, the critical issue is not to direct the neurosciences to the supposedly good or appropriate psychologies, but rather, to sketch out the fundamental aporias, paradoxes and deadlocks of the both inevitable and impossible reliance of neuroscience on psychology. However, here the question could arise, are we, the critics, then saints or prophets, the only ones who see how things really are? But of course, the critics are not the only detached party, the sole ones looking down to the sublunary with wonder or amusement, pity or indulgence. Because when the mists lift at the vantage point, the critics should be able to see that they are in the company of not only the scientists, but also of the so-called laypersons. For, is not the Archimedean point of view, inevitably underpinning both science and the critique of science, eventually shared by the layperson? That is, the human subject can be said to relate to itself, the others and the world via the Other: he or she sees him or herself, the others and the world via the gaze of the Other. Since modernity, this gaze structuring our being with ourselves and the others – and with Being tout-court – is no longer the Divine gaze looking down from the heavens but, rather, the scientific gaze looking down from an alleged objective, equally remote point of view. The modern subject, then, can be said to be *the subject of the sciences*, called upon to understand itself via science and especially via psychology and neuroscience. It is not lonely at the peak of Olympus.

So if Vandenbroeck writes that, concerning the recent neuroturn, the truth claims "have become so dominant that it is now difficult to look at children and early years policies outside of this dominant paradigm" then this holds true not only for professionals but also for laypersons. Via all kinds of channels, educators, parents and the children themselves are instructed and educated into the neuro-paradigm. Everybody is introduced in the correlational scheme of the neuro-psy sciences: parents and children are told that what they feel, know and do is related to the colourful brain scans they are showed in their training, parenting courses and in class itself. Does this not entail that the actual subject is not to be situated at the site of *what it is said to be* but, rather, it dwells at the site where that image is constructed? At the least this means that the adaptations and popularizations calling upon the layperson to adopt the scientific perspective are not secondary to neuroscience itself – and this is precisely where neuroscience is being mixed up with the realm of ideology and biopolitics. Let me delve a bit further in the genealogy of this in the next section.

Psychologization and neurologization: The (bygone?) era of interpellation and biopolitics

The just sketched identification of the layperson with the academic gaze is perhaps the major shift of the genealogical older phenomenon of medicalization (see Vandenbroeck's Foucaultian evocation in chapter 1) to the subsequent phenomena of psychologization and neurologization. In the latter the layperson is most centrally *interpellated*, to use Althusser's term (Althusser, 2006), to subjectivize him or herself via the scientifically constituted knowledge of psychology and neuroscience.[2] But of course, when at a basic level a medical procedure does not require the layperson to know – paracetamol lowers pain and fever independently of us knowing this – it is clear that already in the medicalization of, for example, education and parenting, the administration of knowledge is a crucial part. In the medicalizing procedures Vandenbroeck describes, caregivers (especially mothers) are thus already minimally interpellated and induced into medical knowledge on, for example, hygiene to counter bacterial infections.

These interpellations into academic knowledge, I claim, are central to modern biopolitics as Michel Foucault conceived this. Foucault conceived biopolitics and its advent in the eighteenth century as the trading of centralized sovereign power with dispersed disciplinary mechanisms which for the first time in history centred on the governance of life itself: natural life (bios) came to be included in the mechanisms and calculations of power (Foucault, 1978).[3] Hence the centrality of the sciences of life (both the natural and the human sciences) and the normative concepts that emerge from them begin to structure and determine political action and its goals (Lemke, 2011, p. 33). It is here moreover that for Foucault self-surveillance and self-discipline come in: individual subjects are interpellated to discipline "their own bodies and souls, thoughts, conduct and way of being" (Foucault, 1988, p. 18) by way of adopting the perspective and the normative discourse of the sciences of life and especially the psy- sciences. And although I agree with Vandenbroeck that in modern biopolitics there is a continuity of psychologization with medicalization, I argue that only with psychologization the mechanism of interpellation becomes fully established; only then academic knowledge becomes the crux in the formation of the subject. One could argue that, in the progression of medicalization over psychologization to neurologization, there is a gradual unfolding of what could be called the interpellation of the Enlightenment; remember Immanuel Kant's call to think for oneself. In modernity the final reference of knowledge shifts from tradition and religion to academia. While God's knowledge was unfathomable, mortals remained separated from divine omniscience and omnipotence. When, however, science became the ultimate horizon of knowledge (and hence also of power) the layperson could not remain distinct from both knowledge and power; he or she had to share the knowledge so as to both subjectivize and govern him or herself. Academic knowledge tells you what you are and what you should be.

It is important to see that the centrality of inducing the layperson into the perspective of academia makes that many everyday (inter)subjective practices are closely tied to educational procedures. Parenting, for example, is today clearly connected to manuals, courses and classes. But also children and youngsters are educated in the theories of psychology and neurology so as to deal with their "emotions" and "cognitions". *Neuroeducation*, for that matter, cannot but pass over *neuro-education*; that is, invariably the attempt to underpin schooling and parenting with neuroscience needs the educators, parents and children to be educated in the latest findings of neuroscience (De Vos, 2015; 2016a). Not only grown-ups but also adolescents themselves must, for example, get to know the pubescent brain.[4] Is the radical conclusion not that there is no other way to use psychology and neuroscience for schooling and parenting than bringing them into the curriculum of all parties involved? Already with medicalization, but in a more crystalized way with psychologization and neurologization, the structuring rationale is that of schoolifying the whole of human and social reality.

However, and here I must take my inquiry a decisive step further, is this scheme of the modern subject interpellated into academic knowledge not becoming redundant with the ever growing stronger digital turn? Digitalization – broadly conceived as (inter)subjectivity (our relation with ourselves, the others and the world) more and more passing over digital media and involving data and algorithms – might be considered as a decisive break in the genealogy of medicalization, psychologization and neurologization. Digitalization could be said to fundamentally alter the relation of the subject with knowledge. If the medicalized, psychologized and neurologized subject was interpellated to take upon itself scientific knowledge, then the digitalized subject is not necessarily called upon to share the theoretical outlook; data gathering and handling can function perfectly without a knowing subject. Social media prompt us to like this, to be sorry for that, to remember our mother's birthday, to buy this, without us knowing the coded rationale behind all that. So concerning parenting and education, perhaps there will be less and less need for us (and the children themselves) to be educated in theories about what is driving us: data-technology and algorithms working silently in the background will suffice to drive, guide and steer our behaviour.

Moreover, one should not miss that in the era of Big Data the neuro-psy sciences themselves more and more tend to bypass theory and reflective knowledge as such. As high performance computing is not about knowing or understanding something but about computing and letting the data do the work (see Stiegler, 2015), also the neuro-psy sciences no longer seem to envision a grand knowledge or a grand theory; going more and more digital they suffice gathering alleged primary data, letting computers make inferences and devise pragmatic strategies and protocols.

The European Human Brain Project (HBP) for example aims to "use data-mining techniques to derive an understanding of the way the human brain is constructed and then apply what is learned" (Matthews in: Kandel *et al.*, 2013, p. 659). Hence, eventually it is the computer that understands and "knows", but then in a different way than as we used to know ourselves. Big Neuro-Data even claims to go beyond the neuro-psy correlational scheme I described higher: as Christof Koch a proponent of Big Data neuroscience writes:

> To understand the cerebral cortex, we must bring all available experimental, computational and theoretical approaches to focus on a single model system. In particular, it is of the essence to move from correlation – this neuron or brain region is active whenever the subject does this or that – to causation – this set of molecularly defined neuronal populations is causally involved in that behavior (Koch in: Kandel *et al.*, 2013, p. 660).

Of course, one could contest this and argue that this is still correlational (and theoretical), but the very claim made by Koch is that we are now able to move beyond the different (competing) psychological theories and knowledges and devise a "single model" based purely on data-revealed causation and not on theorized correlation.

Are we thus with digitalization not finally beyond psychologization and neurologization and its interpellative knowledge? If the psy- or neuro-experts claimed insight in the human being and from there turned everybody into their pupils, Big Data as such does not care whether one knows or not: the data-driven so-called *Smart Environments* are more and more able to interact directly and algorithmically with human beings without the mediation of subjectivized knowledge. Here the Foucaultian power/knowledge nexus no longer is operative. Biopolitical power no longer relies on knowing subjects auto-disciplining themselves, rather, via nudging and digital social engineering we are led to do the right thing. So if Henry Markram, one of the principal persons behind the HBP, writes that "The platforms will allow [the neuroscientists] to reconstruct and simulate the brain on supercomputers coupled to virtual bodies acting in virtual environments (in silico behaviour)" (Markram in: Kandel *et al.*, 2013, p. 661), then he misses that such simulation is already at work in the growing digitalization of the lifeworld: a big if not central part of (inter) subjectivity is already about virtual bodies acting in virtual environments.

Is this end of the subject as we knew it, the modern *subject of the sciences* relating to itself, the others and the world via knowledge? Or, concerning parenting and education, is this the end of parents and educators constructing their image of the child and hence of education along the lines of the neuropsychological doxa (and eventually instructing the child itself to adopt the same academic perspective)? As (inter)subjectivity is more and more shaped, steered and conducted in real time via digital nudging technologies, then the digitalization of education and parenting might not need anymore to mobilize subjects interiorizing expert knowledge to look upon oneself, the others and the world. Arguably, we are heading towards algorithmic guided parenting and education bypassing reflexive, psychologized and neurologized subjects. Or might it be that the digi-turn mobilizes or even generates new subject positions, either being still tributary or, in contrast, leaving behind the paradigm of interpellation of medicalized, psychologized and neurologized times. This chapter will, of course, not succeed in answering this as such, but content itself with exploring the grounds and sketching some dynamics involved in what seems to be an important if not decisive transition concerning (inter)subjectivity.

Bring the children to the screen

Education, it can be argued, is about externalization, about bringing the children to the public space. In this respect, any form of public education (in which the community is involved with children and youth) constitutes a transition in time and space of the private to the public. Since modernity the induction into knowledge became most central in this transition. Home and the family provided the rough diamond, to be polished institutionally through discipline (character building) and knowledge transfer. The public sphere, then, was the place where the knowledge had to be applied: the place for a return on investment, where being encultured and educated was validated.[5] Of course, the initial point of departure, the family and the private sphere, should not be seen as natural entities, only subsequently controlled and put to use for political and economic ends. Rather, the categories of the family and the private are social and historical constructions which only saw light in opposition with their alleged outside (the public sphere, the market…).

However, psychologization, especially in its post-World War II intensification (if one allows me this, admittedly, rough historical sketch), could be said to have blurred the formerly strict division between the private and the public. Via processes of psychologization, home and family issues were brought into public education and the school. The latter no longer dealt exclusively with discipline and knowledge transfer but also became in charge of for example everybody's emotional well-being and mental health. If the initial partition could be said to be ideological, the subsequent meshing up was equally so: it aligned the private sphere of the family with the shifting modes of production of post-Fordism. From being the private source of labour force appropriated in capitalism to realize surplus value, the subjective and the personal became directly integrated in post-industrial production and consumption. Arguably, hence, post-Fordism highly leaned on the phenomenon of psychologization (De Vos, 2012), as the latter can be linked directly to the post-Fordist paradigm of the "direct production of subjectivity and social relations" (as in the definition of Hardt & Negri, 2004).

Neurologization, then, effected another turn of the screw: as neuroscience allegedly makes accessible the very hardware of the personal, the private is fully turned inside out and made public. While one can argue that in psychological times the layperson is called upon to adopt the external, and thus public, gaze to contemplate (and hence objectify and commodify) his or her psychic intricacies, with neurologization this gaze receives a very concrete (but paradoxically both material and virtual) object to be casted upon. *Look at this brain-scan*, neuroscience tells us, *this is where your thinking, feeling … actually takes place!* From here the layperson adopts the neuro-knowledge and correlates his or her innermost person to brain areas, neurotransmitters, plasticity and other wonderful things of the brain. Here, the neuroturn even seems to realize an upward mobility: instead of being the hard working labourer of your (intangible) Self, one becomes the entrepreneur, if not stakeholder, of the corporeal brain (the pseudo-concretized You); by taking care of it (eating well, doing brain exercises), the brain will from itself generate the surplus.

However, with digitalization, are the times not bygone of parents bringing their children out into the open via the transitory space of the nursery and the school, and in this way, as per psychologization and neurologization, offering the private to the public market? For, nowadays parents bring their children out into the open more and more via the screen and the network. One could even argue that by introducing their newborn or even unborn on social media (photo or video-wise), parents seek a new way of registering their offspring publicly. Moreover, getting children and even toddlers to the screen and the network as soon as possible (of course with the appropriate caution) has become a widespread public policy.[6] While the advocates of early digital education point to the strengthening of cognitive and motor skills and the fun of actively and creatively engaging with "content" (in contrast to the alleged passivity of knowledge transfer), critics point to negative physical issues (neck and wrists problems, obesitas, sleep problems…), the superficiality of the "learned" content and the social isolation of screen users. But isn't the truly interesting question in this discussion to which space we lead our children?

Most crucially, is the network truly social and public? As has been argued, the virtual world for one person, constituted by his or her particular Facebook page, Twitter account or subscriptions to certain YouTube-channels, is potentially a total different world than for another person. Moreover, as is well known, many websites (news websites for example) adapt their feel, look, content and, of course, their ads to each visitor according to their click and browser history. As we do not necessarily live in the same world, the networked public space risks being the ultimate solipsistic, ersatz and simulacrum-like public sphere. In this respect Christian Fuchs rejects the idealistic interpretations of social media and puts forward a culturalist-materialist understanding: who owns the internet platforms and the social media (Fuchs, 2014)? In the same vein, Geert Lovink urges us to look for the actual power structures involved in social media (Lovink, 2012). Indeed, does our networked virtual lifeworld not boil down to the ultimate blurring of the socio-personal with the corporate, where (inter)subjectivity becomes the central commodity in an unprecedentedly direct and unmediated way, bypassing any transitions in time and space which used to engage a subject interpellated by discipline, knowledge transfer and, consequently, neuropsychological discourses? In Dave Eggers's dystopian novel *The Circle*, one company, after having succeeded in monopolizing all social media and integrating all the different applications in one platform, finally secures that every newborn automatically gets a Circle account, the latter offering the sole access to public services and even being the very tool to cast a vote in, for example, presidential elections (Eggers, 2013). Does this at the least not mean that, potentially, the digitalization of (inter)subjectivity is capable of a more direct enlistment and control of the subject, sidestepping the reflexive and reflective, psychologized and neurologized, knowledgeable and knowing subjectivity of old biopolitics?

At the least the corporatization and privatization, which seems inevitably to come in via digitalization, goes against the grain of the emancipatory envisionings of, for example, Fielding and Moss, who regard common school as a public space "contesting the fragmenting, competitive and selective drive of neoliberal education" (Fielding & Moss, 2012). So if Keri Facer pleads for the physical, local school to be a site "to equip communities to respond to and shape the socio-technical changes" (Facer, 2011, p. 29), the reverse might rather be the reality: the corporate digi-technical shapes the school.

But what, then, becomes of the spaces of early childhood education? The basic idea of the propagators of bringing children and toddlers as soon as possible to the screen is that via the digital and the virtual the "real world" is more accessible and more rapidly brought into education. However, in this rationale and this particular employment of technology in public education, the latter no longer is a temporary transitionary space (the turnstile to the "real world" having itself a certain amplitude) but becomes an empty non-space as it only functions as an interface of the supposedly "real world". Whereas with psychologization and neurologization, the public space of education and schooling became devalued as the private and the corporeal was brought in, with digitalization the threat seems to be that, by bringing the alleged "real world" in as directly accessible, the erstwhile mediatory space of education and schooling is fully encroached and usurped; the once open educational space collapses to a mere empty screen. Put differently, when digital technology is believed to be a direct gateway to the real, education becomes just another app soon to be upgraded or replaced with a newer and faster app. This particular ideology of digital technology moreover not only degrades the public space character of the school, but it also degrades the subjective position of the child or the pupil. The latter becomes a mere node in the network as it is envisioned as an information processing unit in need to be brought in contact with information and data.

All this is grounded in a naturalizing discourse: children are seen as information seeking and digesting creatures, spontaneously inquiring, asking questions and exploring to understand the world (Lind, 1998; Wang et al., 2010). At the same time, we have a naturalization of what parents do; UbicKids, for example, a project aiming to build "smart environments" to assist parenting, describes parenting as "one kind of ordinary human activities" that can be "greatly supported via ubicomp technologies" (Ma et al., 2005, p. 58). Hence, the idea is that what children and parents naturally are and do can be directly addressed by technology; the natural and the artificial seemingly match very well together. UbicKids, for example, aims "to provide ubiquitous natural interactive, even proactive, and further autonomic caring helps or services to them with the right means in the right place at the right time".

What one should not miss here is that the envisioning of the child and of parenting as something natural and proto-technological is mirrored by a remarkable anthropomorphization of the digital and technological. As, for example, Ben Williamson remarks, IBM's foray into digital education is explicitly guided by the idea of "brain-inspired computing" (Williamson, 2015, p. 61). IBM's neuro-imagery is bountiful, as they speak of "neuromorphic hardware", "algorithms that learn", "brain-inspired algorithms", "neurosynaptic chip", etc. (cited in: Williamson, 2015, p. 61). With the sociologist Adrian Mackenzie, we can moreover observe the presence of the older psy-imagery too; IBM and Google's so-called "cognitive infrastructures" are described in terms such as "meaning, perception, sense data, hearing, speaking, seeing, remembering, deciding, and surprisingly, imagining and fantasy":

> the increasing "mindfulness" of the infrastructures under construction at IBM, Google and the like predicate a certain re-concatenation of the world, no longer in the mobile train of experience of people … but instead in the relations mindfully discerned in streams of data (Mackenzie, 2015).

Hence, as the datafication of the lifeworld and subjectivity correlates with the anthropomorphization of the techno-digital and of data, it seems that psychologization and neurologization have shifted from the level of the subject to the level of technology itself. After having psychologized and neurologized parents, educators and children, now it is the computers' turn! So if Williamson prompts us to "investigate what social codes of conduct are written into the code, and to conduct genealogical explorations of the claims that underpin the codifying of conduct in software" (Williamson, 2015, p. 21), it is clear that we especially should look for the neuropsychological codes written into the digital structures that host, shape and guide contemporary (inter)subjectivity. At least, the preliminary conclusion is that digitalization is after all not truly a full break with psychologization and neurologization. Let us explore in the next section if this also means that the interpellated neuropsychological subject has not really left the building.

Interpellation digitally revisited: A minimal subject?

As such, the intertwining of psychologization, neurologization and digitalization can be already inferred from the fact that many critiques on digitalization rely precisely on brain arguments. Steiner-Adair and Barker, for example, aiming at "protecting childhood and family relationships in the digital age", link the use of mobile devices to addiction and substance abuse referring to dopamine, the neurotransmitter regulating the brain's reward and pleasure centres (Steiner-Adair & Barker, 2013). However, is it not clear that this neuro-argument on its turn is contaminated with the digital techno-discourse? For, obviously, the idea that information technology affects our dopamine economy is based on envisioning the brain as living and feeding on information and data. Similarly, endorsing

Steiner-Adair's recommendation to keep mealtimes phone and screen-free, Michael Rich points to "the ritual importance of breaking bread together and talking about your day and the *processing* of experience" (cited in: Novotney, 2016, p. 52, emphasis added). Today, we link psy- and social affairs to the brain and, from there, to the technical-digital paradigm. Consider in this respect again the Human Brain Project's aim to identify the "mathematical principles underlying the relationships between different levels of brain organisation and their role in the brain's ability to acquire, represent and store information" (Walker, 2012, p. 9). The brain here a priori features as an information processor, which of course is handy imagery if one wants to model the brain.

Another, and perhaps more central, aspect of the enmeshment of the neuropsychological and the digital can be inferred from "The Digital Brain Switch", a project funded by the Engineering and Physical Sciences Research Council in the UK. The project studied the changing nature of the work-life balance as a result of digital technologies and was particularly interested in "how people switch between different work-life roles – parent, spouse, friend, co-worker, manager, employee – and how digital technologies either support this or act as a barrier".[7] As it starts from a conception of different identities/roles between which one can *switch*, it already phrases subjectivity in ICT-terms, i.e. the idea of switching between windows and programmes. The solutions are then sought in the same technodigital realm:

> We aimed to give people tools to better understand their own work-life balance and to experiment with different ways of managing their work and life. We imagined a life as an experiment application in which people can test different ways of working and, through the application, collect data over time that will allow them to choose between different working methods.[8]

The bottom-line: life is about collecting data, life is an app? What we should not miss here is that, in the face of digitalization, the layperson is called upon to collect and analyse data, he or she is enjoined to become a data scientist. Are we thus not back with the same scheme of interpellation at work in psychologization and neurologization: understand yourself via (neuro)psychological theory, become your own (neuro)psychologist? This is how the project reports such self-experimenting:

> Alan logs on to the Digital Brain Switch (DBS) application to set up an experiment. He is interested in measuring two variables: his self-reported mood level; and the number of times he switches between email, social networks, work and life during the day. In the experiment set-up, he instructs the DBS application to send him a notification at 10pm every day to report his mood level and switching frequency for one month.[9]

Here two further points become clear, firstly, the digitalization of subjectivity and the lifeworld pass over the neuropsychological discourse (the "mood level"), and secondly, the correlation now at stake is no longer the correlation between the psyche and the brain, but, rather, between the neuropsychological and technodigitality. Digital subjectivity is thus about managing and controlling the relation between the neuropsychological and technodigitality by means of technology itself. We do not have to do the auto-disciplining ourselves, the technology (in our example the DBS application) does this in our place: with digitalization we finally have outsourced the classic self-fashioning and self-modelling of psychologization and neurologization.

However, and here we come to the crux of the matter, does this not mean that after all, precisely in this outsourcing, a minimalistic subject still is in gear, still interpellated by academic knowledge and called upon to adopt the external gaze? Consider in respect how, vis-à-vis the correlation between the neuropsychological and the technological, the DBS project presupposes a structural mismatch:

> We may manage transitions through the use of different technologies or moving between locations, but mental and emotional switches may be more difficult to achieve as quickly or completely. We may experience leakage of emotion across activities. In just "dealing with a quick work email while making the tea" we may under-estimate the impact this will have on our mood.[10]

Most crucially, the actual subject is here not situated at the side of the neuropsychological (the emotional) nor at the side of technodigitality, but rather, the subject is the subject of the gap between the neuropsychological and technodigitality. That is, informed and interpellated by science on the mismatch between the emotional and the technological, the subject contemplates this situation and tries to deal with this via technology itself. It is precisely here that the minimalistic subject, while still interpellated by academic knowledge, can delegate the actual knowing to technological devices.

Consider in the same vein the "EVOZ Smart Parenting device", basically a "smart camera" that allows for "Baby Data Tracking". Feeding, changing, sleeping, milestones and temperature data are collected in a repository allowing parents to share data "with coaches and doctors in both graphical and raw data format".[11] The app provides "accessible parenting information" based on age and data patterns: "videos, quick tips and tricks optimized for mobile device viewing".[12] Science's knowledge no longer needs to be adopted by the subject; it can be almost fully dispatched to technology. But to be clear, perhaps one minimal piece of knowledge has to be assumed or acknowledged by the subject itself: the assuring double credo that the network is like a brain, and vice-versa, that the brain is like a computer, so don't worry, everything is neatly attuned. Hence, if modern subjectivity spawned by the Enlightenment already entailed a minimal subject, having no actual latitude nor weight, contemplating itself, the others and the world from a point of view from nowhere as it is interpellated by science (the latter eventually doing the knowing in the subject's place), then perhaps this minimalization of the subject is coming at its height in digitalization. Put differently: with technodigitality, the retreat of the subject reaches a new zenith point. Just consider that with the EVOZ Smart Parenting device one can even outsource lullabies:

> You have tools at your fingertips to help calm your baby from anywhere:
> control the nightlight, talk or sing to the baby from your phone or play lullabies,
> music and even audiobooks offered in the camera.[13]

What thus remains to be seen is how this intensified outsourcing of subjectivity
relates to contemporary biopolitics.

Conclusion: A psychology come true

> Research during the past 10 years, powered by technology such as functional
> magnetic resonance imaging, has revealed that young brains have both fast-
> growing synapses and sections that remain unconnected. This leaves teens
> easily influenced by their environment and more prone to impulsive beha-
> viour.... Most teenagers don't understand their mental hardwiring, so [Fran-
> ces E.] Jensen (whose laboratory research focuses on newborn-brain injury)
> and David K. Urion (an associate professor of neurology who treats children
> with cognitive impairments like autism and attention deficit disorder) are
> giving lectures at secondary schools and other likely places. They hope to
> inform students, parents, educators, and even fellow scientists about these
> new data, which have wide-ranging implications for how we teach, punish,
> and medically treat this age group. As Jensen told some 50 workshop attendees
> at Boston's Museum of Science in April, "This is the first generation of teen-
> agers that has access to this information, and they need to understand some of
> their vulnerabilities" (Ruder, 2008, p. 8).

In a *Harvard Magazine* article, Debra Bradley Ruder offers a clear picture of the core
paradigm of the application of neuroscience in education: it brings neuroscience in the
classroom making teenagers "learning about the teen brain". However, once again, one
cannot but notice how this article is replete with technodigital imagery: speaking of
connections and mental hardwiring, portraying the brain as something that "processes
information" and claiming that "neural networks that help brain cells (neurons) communicate through chemical signals are enlarging in teen brains" (Ruder, 2008, p. 9).

To understand the vicissitudes of the classic interpellative scheme of psychologization
and neurologization when it enters technodigital times the image of the artist Leslie
Cober-Gentry accompanying Ruder's article might be instructive. It features the
teenage brain suspended in mid-air, mapping, most standardly, issues such as sleep-
deprivation, alcohol (ab)use and impulsivity on the brain. At the bottom of the picture
there is a teacher and a blackboard with the words "Learning about the brain". Most
significantly, there are all sorts of USB and UTP cables coming out of the brain, which,
remarkably, do not run to the teacher but are instead handled by little figures in the
background. Does this not mean that digital technology is bypassing the teacher and
the induction of the pupils into the academic discourse? One could even argue that
the figures handling the wires are not really human agents, but rather "bots" or
pieces of software capable of interacting with humans or even acting as if they were

human.[14] As the figures wear t-shirts on which is written "SU", "CU" or "UC" – indicating their academic status I surmise – they seem to stand for the academically informed but, in the end, automatized procedures and protocols of data gathering and data handling. The crucial question hence is whether current developed "intelligent" software that learn and evolve autonomously and which play a growing role in our everyday life (as code underpinning digital nudging, channeling and directing our desires and behaviour, virtual and real) will not add a new dimension to what has been understood as biopolitics. Are we evolving to what one could call *technologically assisted self-disciplining*, or *automated self-surveillance*? But if Woolley *et al.* write that many bots are built to pass themselves off as human (Woolley *et al.*, 2016), the crucial reason to be raised here is: which (neuro)psychology, then, is used to devise and design the bots that are controlling us? Digitalization in this way realizes and intensifies (neuro)psychologization, perhaps in such a way that, although in continuity with its antecedents, it will have decisive and truly new effects: changing fundamentally the face of the world and radically altering (inter)subjectivity, education, parenting and, for that matter, biopolitics as such.

Consider in this respect the previously mentioned smart parenting project UbicKids. Claiming to realize "a merger of physical and digital spaces" it states that "[o]ne essential feature of ubicomp is to get physical and get real … in everyday life" (Ma *et al.*, 2005, p. 62). The idea here is that digital technology not only can gather and compute data, but from there also can interact with and intervene in the "real world". But how should we understand this intervening and acting upon the real world? Is this "getting physical and real" not in the first instance the altering of reality and the lifeworld according to the pre-formatted models that back up the algorithms in order to guide and steer (inter)subjectivity? That is, instead of simply getting back to the real world, the smart educational and parenting environments are perhaps first and foremost engaged in *shaping the world* in their own image. Or put differently, making an environment smart is above all about spreading a virtual and fictitious garb over "the concrete world". While for example the project UbicKids aims at the outsourcing of certain "tedious and quite stressful" aspects of parenting to digital technology (Ma *et al.*, 2005, p. 60), it wants to open up more space for the things that really matter: "give the family more time to spend with each other" (Ma *et al.*, 2005, p. 65). But how to conceptualize the latter, the so-called "things that matter" if not along the typical mainstream psycho-social models of "quality time", "the sharing of emotions", etc.? In other words, getting real here means the imposing of normative, psychologizing models on reality. The fundamental shift here should not be missed: in pre-digital times (social) psychology was deduced post-factum (with experiments and questionnaires), it was surmised, hypothesized, if not fantasized. As now (inter)subjectivity is given form within the virtual environment based on neuropsychological theories and models, (social) psychology is made "real". Or, the once surmised/fantasized models of (social) neuropsychology become reality passing over virtuality. Here the famous quote of Hannah Arendt concerning behaviourism comes into mind:

The trouble with modern theories of behaviorism is not that they are wrong but that they could become true, that they actually are the best possible conceptualization of certain obvious trends in modern society. It is quite conceivable that the modern age – which began with such an unprecedented and promising outburst of human activity – may end in the deadliest, most sterile passivity history has ever known (Arendt, 1958, p. 322).

Hence, similarly, the trouble with (neuro)psychology is not that it would be wrong, but that it would become true via the virtualization of our lifeworld. *Biopolitics 2.0*, firmly interlocking the psychological, the neurological and the digital, modelling, tracking and coding (inter)subjectivity, might hence lead humanity to an unprecedented deadly and sterile passivity.

A poignant example of the biopolitical intertwining of psychologization, neurologization and the digitalization of (inter)subjectivity, the parenting app Vroom starts from the recent revived interest in attachment theories:

New science tells us that our children's first years are when they develop the foundation for all future learning. Every time we connect with them, it's not just their eyes that light up – it's their brains too. In these moments, half a million neurons are at once, taking in all the things we say and do. We can't see it happening, but it's all there, all at work. That's why Vroom is here.[15]

Clearly, to begin with, attachment came back into attention via the neuroturn as attachment is claimed to be made tangible by digital brain imaging techniques, or psychological speculations made substantial by fleshing them out via the brains scan.[16] But the true substantialization is the ensuing one: that is the biopolitical realization of the mainstream card-board psychologies via the digitalization of everyday life:

Vroom turns shared moments into brain building moments. Whether it's mealtime, bathtime, or anytime in between, there are always ways to nurture our children's growing minds.[17]

The digitalization of (inter)subjectivity confirms, builds on and expands the biopolitics of psychologization and neurologization and does this in truly novel ways. It yet remains to be seen how deep the rabbit hole goes and what will be the vicissitudes of the left behind, minimal subject.

Notes

1 See also my chapter "The Political Brain" in De Vos, 2016b.
2 So indeed, as Vandenbroeck has it, the layperson cannot see, but it is precisely here that he/she is called upon to adopt the gaze of science which claims to see how things are. Neuroscience's *"look, this is what you are"* invites the layperson to identify not as such with the thing of the brain but, rather with – and here I subvert the classic Althusserian scheme – the scientific perspective: *can I have a look, is this what I am?*

3 "For millennia, man remained what he was for Aristotle: a living animal with the additional
   capacity for a political existence; modern man is an animal whose politics places his existence
   as a living being in question" (Foucault, 1978, p. 143).
4 See for example: http://www.heysigmund.com/the-adolescent-brain-what-they-need-
   to-know/.
5 While arguably class plays a central role here, classic liberal-capitalist ideology envisions
   the public space as an egalitarian ground allowing socio-economic mobility.
6 See for example The Creative Classrooms Lab project: http://creative.eun.org/home.
7 http://www.scc.lancs.ac.uk/research/projects/DBS/.
8 http://www.scc.lancs.ac.uk/research/projects/DBS/.
9 http://www.scc.lancs.ac.uk/research/projects/DBS/.
10 http://www.scc.lancs.ac.uk/research/projects/DBS/wp-content/uploads/2015/06/
   DBS-A2-CMYK-fold-to-A4-FINAL.pdf.
11 https://www.evozbaby.com/.
12 The concept of interpassivity developed by Robert Pfaller (2000) could here come in
   mind!
13 https://www.evozbaby.com/.
14 "Bots measure the technical health of the Internet, share information on natural disasters,
   predict disease outbreaks, fulfill our lunch requests, and send news articles to networks of
   people on platforms like Twitter and Slack. They may even write some of those articles.
   They are also integral to social media propaganda campaigns, distributed denial of service
   (DDoS) attacks, and stock market manipulation. Bots have been shown to be capable of
   compelling humans to carry out small tasks, and a 'Siri-like' assistant has been proposed as a
   way to reduce 'moral injury' when drone pilots fire on their targets" (Woolley et al., 2016).
15 http://www.joinvroom.org/.
16 Davi Thornton already perspicuously pointed to the biopolitical aspects of the technologically mediated revival of attachment: underpinned by the authority of brain science,
   attachment opens up as field of government: "a locus for the cultivation and distribution
   of disciplinary practices mothers are induced to take up. ... Because of the modes of
   visualization offered by brain imaging, these practices are subject to various measure-
   ments, calculations, and calibrations: different aspects of mothering can be quantified and
   temporally regulated according to precise equations" (Thornton, 2011, p. 411).
17 http://www.joinvroom.org/.

References

Althusser, L. (2006). Ideology and ideological state apparatuses (notes towards an investiga-
   tion). In S. Aradhana & G. Akhil (Eds.), *The anthropology of the state: A reader* (pp. 86–111).
   Malden, MA: Blackwell Publishing.
Arendt, H. (1958). *The human condition*. Chicago, IL: University of Chicago Press.
De Vos, J. (2012). *Psychologisation in times of globalisation*. London: Routledge.
De Vos, J. (2015). Deneurologizing education? From psychologisation to neurologisation
   and back. *Studies in Philosophy and Education,* 34(3), 279–295. doi:10.1007/s11217-014-
   9440-5
De Vos, J. (2016a). The death and the resurrection of (psy)critique: The case of neuroedu-
   cation. *Foundations of Science*, 21(1), 129–145.
De Vos, J. (2016b). *The metamorphoses of the brain. Neurologization and its discontents*. New
   York: Palgrave Macmillan.
Eggers, D. (2013). *The circle*. New York: Knopf.
Facer, K. (2011). *Learning futures: Education, technology and social change*. London: Routledge.
Fielding, M., & Moss, P. (2012). Radical democratic education. Paper presented at the
   annual conference of the American Sociological Association, Denver, Colorado.

Foucault, M. (1978). *The history of sexuality*, vol. 1 (R. Hurley, Trans.). New York: Vintage.

Foucault, M. (1988). Technologies of the self. In L. H. Martin, H. Gutman & P. H. Hutton (Eds.), *Technologies of the self: A seminar with Michel Foucault* (pp. 16–49). Amherst: University of Massachusetts Press.

Fuchs, C. (2014). Social media and the public sphere. *Communication, Capitalism & Critique*, 12(1), 57–101.

Hardt, M., & Negri, A. (2004). *Multitude*. New York: The Penguin Press.

Kandel, E. R., Markram, H., Matthews, P. M., Yuste, R., & Koch, C. (2013). Neuroscience thinks big (and collaboratively). *Nature Reviews Neuroscience*, 14(9), 659–664.

Lemke, T. (2011). *Biopolitics: An advanced introduction*. New York: New York University Press.

Lesnik-Oberstein, K. (2015). Motherhood, evolutionary psychology and mirror neurons or "Grammar is politics by other means". *Feminist Theory*, 16(2), 171–187.

Lind, K. K. (1998). Science in early childhood: Developing and acquiring fundamental concepts and skills. Paper presented at the Forum on Early Childhood Science, Mathematics, and Technology Education on February 6–8. Washington, DC: National Science Foundation.

Lovink, G. (2012). What is the social in social media? *E-Flux Journal*, 40.

Ma, J., Yang, L. T., Apduhan, B. O., Huang, R., Barolli, L., & Takizawa, M. (2005). Towards a smart world and ubiquitous intelligence: A walkthrough from smart things to smart hyperspaces and UbicKids. *International Journal of Pervasive Computing and Communications*, 1(1), 53–68.

Mackenzie, A. (2015). Demis Hassabis: Mindful infrastructures and re-concatenated worlds. Retrieved from http://rian39.github.io/infrastructure/2015/02/06/Demis-Hassabis-Mindful-Infrastructures.html.

Novotney, A. (2016). Smartphone=not-so-smart parenting? *Monitor on Psychology*, 47(2), 52.

Pfaller, R. (2000). *Interpassivität: Studien über delegiertes genießen*. Wien/New York: Springer.

Ruder, D. B. (2008). The teen brain. *Harvard Magazine*, 111(1), 8–10.

Steiner-Adair, C., & Barker, T. H. (2013). *The big disconnect: Protecting childhood and family relationships in the digital age*. New York: Harper Business.

Stiegler, B. (2015). *La Société automatique: 1. L'avenir du travail*. Paris: Fayard.

Thornton, D. J. (2011). Neuroscience, affect, and the entrepreneurialization of motherhood. *Communication and Critical/Cultural Studies*, 8(4), 399–424.

Walker, R. (2012). The Human Brain Project: A report to the European Commission. Retrieved from https://www.humanbrainproject.eu/documents/10180/17648/TheHBPReport_LR.pdf/18e5747e-10af-4bec-9806-d03aead57655.

Wang, F., Kinzie, M. B., McGuire, P., & Pan, E. (2010). Applying technology to inquiry-based learning in early childhood education. *Early Childhood Education Journal*, 37(5), 381–389.

Williamson, B. (Ed.) (2015). *Coding/learning: Software and digital data in education*. Stirling, UK: University of Stirling.

Woolley, S., Boyd, D., Broussard, M., Elish, M., Fader, L., Hwang, T., … Shorey, S. (2016). How to think about bots: A botifesto. Retrieved from http://motherboard.vice.com/read/how-to-think-about-bots.

Žižek, S. (2010). *Living in the end times*. London/New York: Verso.

3

USING YOUR BRAIN

Child development, parenting and politics of evidence

Sue White and Dave Wastell

This chapter will examine the processes through which neuroscientific knowledge makes its way into social policy and professional practice, bringing with it significant implications for the relationship between the state and the family. The chapter picks up themes from the introduction to this book, particularly focusing on the turn to economic forms of thought and the rise of expert discourses, so that the solution to social problems are rendered technical and obscured from lay scrutiny. We draw on our previous work (Wastell and White, 2012; White and Wastell, 2013; White and Wastell, 2016; Wastell and White, 2017) to provide a summary of the origins of the current neuroenthusiasm, using current UK early years policy as a case study. We consider the manner in which policy makers typically make use of neuroscientific and other expert evidence. Neuroscientific understandings are also working their way into professional practice, in early years provision and child and family social work in particular. We illustrate our arguments with two exemplars from recent social policy in the UK, which we think are harbingers of what may swiftly be coming to other parts of Europe.

Beginning in the USA with the "decade of the brain", launched by George Bush in 1990, social policy enthusiastically conscripted neuroscience to its projects. Neuroscience is modern; it is very *now*. Rose (2010) traces the arrival of brain science from the European side of the Atlantic to an agenda passionately promoted by Ian Duncan-Smith, a senior figure and former leader of the UK Conservative Party, and his unlikely ally from the Labour Party, Graham Allen. They joined forces in 2008 to produce a report, *Early Intervention: Good Parents, Great Kids, Better Citizens* (Allen and Smith, 2009), in which the line of argumentation developed in two subsequent reports (Allen, 2011a, 2011b; discussed in detail below) makes its first appearance: "the structure of the developing infant brain is a crucial factor in the creation (or not) of violent tendencies" (Allen and Smith, 2009: 57). Thus, criminality is depicted as hard-wired in the brain, and acting with alacrity in its prevention is a self-evident moral imperative. If brains can be boosted, why not boost them!

In 2010, another Labour MP, Frank Field, entered the fray. Again, the aspiration was to end poverty and disadvantage. The medium through which this would be accomplished was the infant brain.

> The development of a baby's brain is affected by the attachment to their parents and analysis of neglected children's brains has shown that their brain growth is significantly reduced. Where babies are often left to cry, their cortisol levels are increased and this can lead to a permanent increase in stress hormones later in life, which can impact on mental health. Supporting parents during this difficult transition period is crucial to improving outcomes for young children (Field, 2010: 43).

In recent years we have increasingly seen a shift in the policy rhetoric in the UK from a focus on prevention to more coercive and controlling social engineering by the state, as we can see in the following extract from David Cameron's (then UK prime minister) speech on "life chances":

> Thanks to the advent of functional MRI scanners, neuroscientists and biologists say they have learnt more about how the brain works in the last 10 years than in the rest of human history. And one critical finding is that the vast majority of the synapses ... develop in the first 2 years. Destinies can be altered for good or ill in this window of opportunity ... we know the severe developmental damage that can be done ... when babies are emotionally neglected, abused or if they witness domestic violence. As Dr Jack Shonkoff's research at Harvard University has shown, children who suffer what he calls "toxic stress" in those early years are potentially set up for a life of struggle, risky behaviour, poor social outcomes, all driven by abnormally high levels of the stress hormone, cortisol (11th January 2016).[1]

We note in all these proclamations the complete absence of any doubt about the precariousness of the infant brain, or the permanence of the "damage" which may ensue from suboptimal parenting. Brains become perfectible and thus must be perfected. The reader has already encountered the Harvard Center on the Developing Child in the introduction to this collection and will recall the sophisticated messaging and artful simplification of research involved in producing a "core story" of development. We will revisit the Harvard Center in due course, but for now we must note that this kind of translation, or traduction, of science is pivotal to it packing a policy punch. It is worth examining what we know about how policy makers use research.

Making the core neuro-developmental story

"Evidence" for policy making is not sitting in journals ready to be harvested by assiduous systematic reviewers. Rather, it is dynamically created through the human interaction around the policy making table ... achieved mostly through dialogue, argument, influence and conflict and retrospectively made sense of through the telling of stories (Greenhalgh and Russell, 2006: 36).

As Greenhalgh and Russell note, "evidence" in the policy world knowledge is actively *made*. In an ethnographic study of the use of evidence in UK policy making, Stevens (2011) describes how civil servants are routinely faced with rather too much evidence, very little of which provides clear answers to the specific policy question before them. Their sense of personal career success and their hopes for promotion depend on the government of the day accepting their proposals as policy. A good deal of the civil servants' day is spent in discussion and argument with others within the state machine; crafting persuasive stories is central. Stevens tells of the process whereby a document he had drafted, on an area of considerable academic uncertainty, was subject to many weeks of revision. All the caveats and references to areas of unsettled knowledge were gradually removed. When the document was finally passed to another department, heated concerns were raised that it conflicted with a previously published document. In the final version, the headline estimate of a previously published report was used, obviating the need for supporting data. Any surviving caveats were relegated to an appendix.

> [U]ncertainty was seen ... as the enemy of policy-making. ... My discussion of caveats ... was characterised by our team leader ... as "verging in the philosophical". He evidently saw them as an obstacle to the practical issue of what action to take, right here, right now (Stevens, 2011: 243).

The use of neuroscience in policy has been explored specifically by Broer and Pickersgill (2015), who interviewed policy makers in Scotland. They show how opinion formers use science to give authority to policies which they feel are politically and morally right:

> Well you know, if you tell a society that the way in which they nurture children changes the way their brains develop, and you show them pictures that corroborate that, it's pretty compelling. No one wants to damage a child's brain, or to deny a child the opportunity to develop their brain properly. It's emotive, and it's powerful (p. 55).

Whilst some of their respondents were cautious about applications of neuroscience, others engaged self-consciously in "pragmatic reductionism" (p. 59) – evidence was self-consciously stripped of any equivocation. It was rendered into simplified form, "packaged" to persuade. One of their respondents explains:

> What we do is condense all the findings and say these are the kind of key findings, right. What we then don't do, is go, but this person thinks it's ridiculous because it doesn't show x, y or z ... this has only been done with middle class

parents or these people think it's not valid because it wasn't done with a controlled group etc. ... because otherwise we would just confuse people (p. 61).

Translations have had to take place to render the science settled and clear. When facts have already been pre-packed, simplified and turned into a ready meal elsewhere, as is the case with the Harvard Center, the policy makers have precisely what they need. Indeed, the purpose of the Harvard site was precisely to address the penchant for sound bite science amongst politicians and their policy mandarins. On tracing the history of the Harvard Center, it becomes apparent that their work of "clear dissemination" is actually a skilful and co-ordinated act of persuasion, involving collaboration with FrameWorks Institute, a communications company. In a peer reviewed paper, one of the founders of the Harvard Center explains:

> Science has an important role to play in advising policymakers on crafting effective responses to social problems that affect the development of children. This article describes lessons learned from a multiyear, working collaboration among neuroscientists, developmental psychologists, paediatricians, economists, and communications researchers who are engaged in the iterative construction of a core story of development, using simplifying models (i.e., metaphors) such as "brain architecture," "toxic stress," and "serve and return" to explain complex scientific concepts to non-scientists (Shonkoff and Bales, 2011: 17).

The aspirations of this extended, cross disciplinary project were thus to produce a faithful translation of the science, aiming to create a public sense of shared responsibility for children and for strategic investment in their future. The tone is communitarian not totalitarian. Nevertheless, the production of a "core story" required the development of a new metaphorical vocabulary. The processes by which this was achieved were complex, drawing on anthropology, cognitive science and linguistics to map "conceptual models" in public use, synthesizing these with expert knowledge to develop "powerful frame cues" (Shonkoff and Bales, 2011: 20) in the form of metaphors and values. Expert knowledge was recast into folk understandings, various things were no longer bad just because they were bad, but because they damage children's brains. The stage was thus set for the "core story" to inform policy and crucially professional practice, not only in terms of family support, but also at the more coercive end of the state apparatus.

At this point we shall examine our first exhibit to show how the science was used and abused in the UK, in Graham Allen's influential reports on "early intervention".

Graham Allen and neurosocial policy: Does the evidence matter?

> [B]abies are born with 25 per cent of their brains developed, and there is then a rapid period of development so that by the age of 3 their brains are 80 per cent developed. In that period, neglect, the wrong type of parenting and other adverse experiences can have a profound effect on how children are emotionally "wired" (Allen, 2011a: xiii).

In Allen's interim report (2011a), published in January 2011, the brain is mentioned 59 times, and the front cover carries dramatic images, which have become ubiquitous in child welfare texts, of an infant brain damaged by neglect. Allen's second report, published in the summer of 2011, retains the brain image on the cover, now joined by symbolic bars of gold emphasizing the economic sense behind "early intervention" (Allen, 2011b). Saliently, the brain is not mentioned in the second report; the case having been made, it is now simply a question of taking action. Allen goes on to propose various preferred ways whereby the social ills of disadvantaged families may, he believes, be remedied. Advocated are a range of "evidence based", time limited, targeted interventions into "parenting", to be delivered in a "payment by results" regime; these are also the preferred instruments commended by Field in his report of 2010.

The brain images on the front cover are potent. How could the State not act swiftly to prevent such an atrocity? But all is not as it seems. First, we shall inspect the narrative of the Report, beginning in chapter 1, where the neuroscientific case for early intervention starts to take shape. Paragraph 17 (page 6) states:

> The early years are far and away the greatest period of growth in the human brain. It has been estimated that the connections or synapses in a baby's brain grow 20-fold, from having perhaps 10 trillion at birth to 200 trillion at age 3. For a baby, this is an explosive process of learning from the environment. The early years are a very sensitive period when it is much easier to help the developing social and emotional structure of the infant brain, and after which the basic architecture is formed for life. However, it is not impossible for the brain to develop later, but it becomes significantly harder, particularly in terms of emotional capabilities, which are largely set in the first 18 months of life.

Here Allen draws on what Bruer (1999) has called the "myth of the first three years". The idea that the first three years (or "1001 days") determine the rest of the child's life provides the "core story of development" forming the basis for much of the moral case for early intervention. Bruer's critique of the myth of the first three years has been briefly touched on in other chapters of this book. In summary, he identifies three neuroscience strands underpinning the myth. First, the idea that the early years represent a period of "biological exuberance" in the development of brain connectivity is only part of the story. The number of synapses subsequently reaches a plateau, followed by synaptic pruning in which densities decline to adult levels, i.e. at the point in adolescence when humans begin to learn and master increasingly complex bodies of knowledge, their synapses are undergoing mass elimination.

Bruer goes on to attack the concept of the "critical period". Rather than such immutable windows, neuroscience actually shows the brain to be highly plastic and adaptable. Bruer demonstrates this through research on language acquisition, where critical periods are the exception, not the rule; he also draws attention to the capacity of the human for life-long learning to deconstruct the idea that critical periods are the norm. The third strand of the myth is the idea that enriched, more stimulating environments augment brain development, boosting "brain power". Although the brains of rats reared in complex laboratory environments (large cages with companions, toys, etc.) show increased synaptic density, compared to rats brought up in isolation and cramped conditions, drilling into the experimental detail of the seminal studies reveals that the period of deprivation extended well into advanced childhood in human terms. Moreover, increases in dendritic density from "enriched experience" can be shown at any age. The conditions experienced by the rats were also somewhat extreme compared to any plausible human situation; reading "Palo Alto" for complex and "South Bronx" for isolated is somewhat simplistic. Bruer then turns his critical gaze on early-intervention programmes for children, such as North Carolina Abecedarian Project. Whilst such interventions often show initial benefits, these rapidly diminish over time and have largely disappeared by mid-adolescence; duration, timing and programme content are also inextricably confounded in such interventions, making it impossible to draw clear conclusions regarding the criticality of the early years.

Despite its importance and relevance, the Allen reports pay no attention to Bruer's thorough and respected critique; it is not mentioned at all. This neglect exemplifies the policy-making behaviours we discussed at the start of this chapter: the imperative is to persuade, not to present faithfully the state of the scientific field. The Report is a particularly egregious example of the rhetorical use of scientific research; it does not really matter what the research papers say, so long as the brain is mentioned. Chapter 2 of the first Allen Report, entitled "Using our brains", purports to provide a detailed elaboration of the neuroscientific evidence. Its epigraph provides an instructive example of the modus operandi:

> A lack of appropriate experiences can lead to alterations in genetic plans. Moreover, although the brain retains the capacity to adapt and change throughout life, this capacity decreases with age.[3]

The reader will spot the superscript 3 at the end of the second sentence. Such numbered citations implicitly construct the report as an academically rigorous piece of writing. But when the end-note is checked, an altogether different picture emerges. The endnote invokes three journal articles; the titles of these are as follows: "Adaptive auditory plasticity in developing and adult animals"; "Cortical plasticity: from synapses to maps"; "Experience-dependent plasticity in the adult visual cortex". Given the volume of neuroscience research stretching over several decades, with much of it bearing directly on Allen's claim, this is a puzzling selection. Why these three papers? Even the titles suggest an uneasy fit with the report's thesis, all mentioning "plasticity", and two in the context of the adult brain. In fact, the titles accurately reflect what the neuroscience overwhelmingly shows; namely, a plastic, adaptable nervous system, not a brain "formed for life".

Into the neuroscience soon is woven Attachment Theory. The importance of secure attachment is invoked (p. 13):

> Children develop in an environment of relationships that usually begin within their family. From early infancy, they naturally reach out to create bonds, and they develop best when caring adults respond in warm, stimulating and consistent ways. This secure attachment with those close to them leads to the development of empathy, trust and well-being.

Strong claims are then made regarding long-term effects of such early attachment patterns, especially the beneficial effects of secure attachment and the adverse impact of failing to make such bonds (Allen, 2011a: p. 15).

> Recent research also shows insecure attachment is linked to a higher risk for a number of health conditions, including strokes, heart attacks and high blood pressure, and suffering pain, for example from headaches and arthritis.
> Huntsinger and Luecken showed that people with secure attachment show more healthy behaviours such as taking exercise, not smoking, not using substances and alcohol, and driving at ordinary speed.

The impression is again created of enduring damage caused by early deficits. Once more it is important to read the "journal science", i.e., the original research papers. Two studies are cited (McWilliams and Bailey, 2010; Huntsinger and Luecken, 2004) as the basis for the quoted claims. However, these are not studies of children, but of adults, using "attachment style" as a way of conceptualizing the adult personality assessed, using self-report questionnaires. The various behaviours mentioned in the second study (exercise, smoking, etc.) refer to answers to another questionnaire. The study does not directly address the lasting damage of insecure attachment in infants; it simply shows that students with "secure style of interaction with loved ones" also describe themselves as engaging in generally "healthier health behavior" (p. 523). Neither shows, nor purports to show, any link with early childhood experiences.

In subsequent paragraphs of the Report, damaged emotionality and damaged brains come together, and the source of both is attributed to deficient parenting (p. 15):

> Parents who are neglectful or who are drunk, drugged or violent, will have impaired capacity to provide this social and emotional stability, and will create the likelihood that adverse experiences might have a negative impact on their children's development as they mature. Although poor parenting practices can cause damage to children of all ages, the worst and deepest damage is done to children when their brains are being formed during their earliest months and years. The most serious damage takes place before birth and during the first 18 months of life.

The only evidence invoked by Allen for these broad and portentous claims is the prenatal abuse of alcohol: "Fetal Alcohol Spectrum Disorder", a rather limited and extreme basis for drawing such wide-ranging implications. Let us now look more deeply into the source of the iconic brain images on the Report's cover. They are attributed to the Child Trauma Academy (www.childtrauma.org), a campaigning "child advocacy" organization led by Bruce Perry. A reference is given to an article published by Perry in 2002. The key section of the paper (p. 92) is less than a page long, with scant methodological and clinical detail, such as "History was obtained from multiple sources (investigating CPS workers, family, and police)." The paper covers alleged impact of neglect on brain development and the two main groups of cases compared are children suffering from "global neglect" (history of sensory deprivation in more than one domain, e.g., minimal exposure to language, physical contact or social interaction); and "chaotic neglect". Perry's main result is that the head sizes for the globally neglected children were extremely small, whereas those suffering from chaotic neglect fell in the normal range.

> Furthermore in cases where MRI or CT scans were available, neuroradiologists interpreted 11 of 17 scans as abnormal from the children with global neglect (64.7%) and only 3 of 26 scans as abnormal from the children with chaotic neglect (11.5%). The majority of the readings were "enlarged ventricles" or "cortical atrophy" (see Figure 1).

A book focused on translating neuroscience for social workers (Farmer, 2009) provides further evidence of how compelling brain images can be. Figure 5.2 in Farmer contains a set of three pairs of images reproduced from Perry's website. Critical comment is absent: the figure legend merely contains the phrase "severe sensory deprivation in early childhood". Each pair juxtaposes a damaged brain with the "normal brain" of another child, although the basis for the pairing is not explained. The three normal brains are themselves all somewhat different; one indeed, is much the same size as one of the neglected brains. There are numerous other instances of the use of such images, and the work from which they originate, being recruited by the campaigners. We remarked in the introduction to this chapter that Perry's work is the only evidence advanced in Frank Field's report to support his "brain damage" argument. The images used by Allen also make their appearance in a document designed to guide professional decision-making by family judges in cases involving the children at risk, which we discuss later in the chapter.

Returning to the Allen Report, the infant brain and its terrible vulnerabilities are invoked again. The following paragraphs summarize the general thrust of Allen's argument:

> Different parts of the brain ... develop in different sensitive windows of time. The estimated prime window for emotional development is up to 18 months, by which time the foundation of this has been shaped by the way in which the prime carer interacts with the child. ... Infants of severely depressed mothers

show reduced left lobe activity (associated with being happy, joyful and interested) and increased right lobe activity (associated with negative feelings). These emotional deficits are harder to overcome once the sensitive window has passed (Allen, 2011a: 16).

If the predominant early experience is fear and stress, the neurochemical responses to those experiences become the primary architects of the brain. Trauma elevates stress hormones, such as cortisol. One result is significantly fewer synapses (or connections). Specialists viewing CAT scans of the key emotional areas in the brains of abused or neglected children have likened the experience to looking at a black hole. In extreme cases the brains of abused children are significantly smaller than the norm, and the limbic system (which governs the emotions) may be 20–30 per cent smaller and contain fewer synapses (ibid: 16).

Again, we shall look more closely at the neuroscience evidence invoked in the first paragraph. The research cited is a paper by Dawson *et al.* (1994), which examines patterns of scalp-recorded brain activity (the EEG) associated with emotional disturbances in the children of depressed mothers. Dawson's experimental evidence actually goes in the opposite direction to that claimed in the Report. Referring to the distressed reactions of children when mothers left the room, the EEG response is described as follows: "the infants of symptomatic mothers exhibited an unexpected pattern of greater left than right activation during the maternal separation condition" (ibid: 772). More "positive" emotion it would seem.

In sum, we contend that the Allen Report uses two recurrent devices to misrepresent the neuroscientific knowledge-base. First, its instability, uncertainty and contradictions are not disclosed; it is presented as a settled, incontrovertible consensus: "We now know, etc., etc." Second, from the vast neuroscientific literature, papers are tendentiously selected to support policy positions, even though they often do not. The insights from the studies of the policy making process, referred to at the start of the chapter, perhaps make these choices less perplexing. Finding evidence for policy can be something of a fishing expedition. Persuasiveness, not accuracy is the primary criterion at work. The evidence has been shaped to support an *a priori* conviction; hence little argumentation is required to make it work rhetorically. The Report does not provide a particularly distinguished exemplar of the public use of science. Rather, science has been conscripted to grant authority to the cause of early intervention; "pragmatic reductionism" has taken place to make this message powerful (Broer and Pickersgill, 2015). This is bolstered by a strong belief that the moral message is bigger than the science.

As is discussed in the introduction to this volume, contemporary settlements about parenting and its role in the production of social ills have a long history; the enrolment of contemporary "biotechnoscience" has made their passage into policy somewhat charmed, giving powerful weight to the argument for resources to intervene early in the lives of disadvantaged children. Given the climate of retrenched services and constrained resources across Europe, the Allen Report has been remarkably successful in promoting this agenda and has been much lauded as a result. But, such a line of reasoning carries consequences which are not so benign as the intentions of its advocates. It extends the gaze of the State and it challenges the category "normal". Normal is no longer normal. In its place, we have optimization as the business of the State. Across the gamut of policy and professional practice, social disadvantage is being recast as a biological effect, curable by professional interventions at the level of individuals, to be implemented across a range of early years services and infant education programmes. As Edwards *et al.* (2015) note:

> The interviews with early years practitioners for our study show that there is also a practice emphasis on the significance of the mother's brain as potentially producing too much of the stress hormone cortisol in pregnancy. ... After birth, mothers also needed to protect their baby from biological risk through inattention and/or rearing them in a difficult environment. ... This concern about cortisol levels positions mothers as in control of their stress reactions, and was expressed through appeals to consider what getting stressed might do to their baby ante and post natally. Practitioners seem to be encouraged to conceptualise stress primarily in terms of relationships rather than pressures associated with disadvantage or lack of resources (Edwards *et al.*, 2015: 177–178).

Thus, it is clear that policy makers are not the only neuro-enthusiasts. Professionals are increasingly incorporating neuroscience into their everyday vocabularies of risk. The following quotation from a recent research interview one of us has undertaken with a family support worker as part of an international study on social workers' understandings of family complexity is typical:

> I mean again if you look at brain development and 0–3 being the most crucial point in their brain development and so the opportunity you've got, and it's a wonderful opportunity, and another, the teenage years, to make some changes but sometimes, certainly their behaviours are entrenched and we can't change them.[2]

Here we can see the recurrent motifs of the neuroscientific thought style, the "critical" first three years, the impossibility of later change and the goal of economic optimization.

Disadvantage is thus re-positioned as a biological phenomenon. Such narratives are equally potent when they shift from campaigns to procure resources for socially deprived groups, to the aspiration to guide professional judgement in individual child protection cases. At this point, we present our next exhibit, a report designed to support decision making in public law cases in the English family courts, which deal with the compulsory removal of children from their families.

From early intervention to child protection: Support or coercion?

In the context of supportive early help, the neuroscientific arguments, however traduced, may be seen as part of a progressive mission to make the world a better place. That is how they are routinely sold by the Harvard site and others. The very same arguments, however, can be mobilized in support of the more coercive activities of the State (Featherstone *et al.*, 2014). Alongside the attention to primary prevention, the UK has a policy allowing the permanent removal and placement for adoption of children without parental consent, pejoratively dubbed by its critics "forced adoption". Early intervention and non-consensual adoption may seem poles apart, but they are often closely related in terms of their supporting discourses. In 2015, UK adoption policy received criticism from the Council of Europe. It was specifically criticized by the Council for its removal of children from women who have been subject to domestic abuse, or who are suffering from depression; in short, those mothers who may also be potential beneficiaries of "early intervention" strategies. These trends continued to accelerate as Fenton Glynn (2015) notes:

> In the year ending 31 March 2014, 5,050 children were adopted from public care, an increase of 26% from 2013, and of 58% from 2010. Adoptions are now at their highest point since the start of complete collection of data (p. 20).

The removals of infants at birth has shown a particularly steep rise (Broadhurst *et al.*, 2015a; Broadhurst *et al.*, 2015b). The president of the Family Division, Judge James Munby, notes the shift in the profile of children placed for adoption: "the typical adoption today is of a child who has been made the subject of a care order … and where parental consent has been dispensed with."[3] Moreover, The Children and Families Act limits the duration of care proceedings (proceedings to remove a child deemed to be at risk from their family) in England and Wales, in all but "exceptional cases" to 26 weeks' duration. Achieving this in congested family courts was bound to be both complex and contentious, with concerns for family rights (particularly in a climate of reduced funding for legal aid) vying with discourses of child-centredness (both articulated in the name of social justice) over the imposition of tight timescales. January 2016 ushered in the announcement of further reforms to adoption law to achieve an increase in numbers. The inference being that we most definitely need more.

The action plan for the implementation of the family justice reforms was the establishment of a "knowledge hub", and the production of a set of knowledge reviews to guide judicial decision making. "Decision making within a child's timeframe: An overview of current research evidence for family justice professionals concerning child development and the impact of maltreatment" (hereafter abbreviated to "A Child's Timeframe") by Rebecca Brown and Harriet Ward (Brown and Ward, 2013), of the University of Loughborough, was one such review and made extensive use of neuroscientific claims. The report was commissioned by the Department for Education and the Family Justice Council. It explicitly stated its purpose as ensuring "consistent training … for family justice professionals". It contains a number of strands, and neuroscience figures strongly in its core argument: namely that "time frames for intervening … are out of kilter with those of the child" (p. 8).

As family lawyer, Eddie Lloyd-Jones (2013) noted in the journal *Family Law*, shortly after the publication of "A Child's Timeframe":

> An email circulated by a designated family judge ... left no one in any doubt as to the status of this document. All needed to be familiar with its contents upon which courts were likely to place "considerable reliance". The report ... is used in judicial training and one participant has already observed that it is treated as "completely authoritative" (Lloyd-Jones, 2013: 1053).

At this point, we review events which took place at the time, as we were involved in a debate with the report's authors shortly after its publication. The controversy that followed is worthy of examination in its own right, attesting to the fact that debates about parenting, childhood vulnerability and state arouse the passions. Here we focus on the argumentation within the review, on our counter argument and the case mobilized in the response from the report's authors that followed. Our summary of the debate provides evidence of the difficulties besetting the search for solid ground on which to base complex professional judgements about children deemed to be at risk, and illustrates the effects of the neurobiological way of thinking.

Contending the core story

Early in 2013, we were contacted by a number of family lawyers who had received the compulsory training to which Lloyd-Jones refers. We had recently published a paper analysing the neuroscientific claims in the Allen Reports (Wastell and White, 2012) and the lawyers were seeking an opinion on the status of the evidence in "A Child's Timeframe". There was concern expressed by some lawyers that the report would lead to the removal of infants on the *precautionary principle*, in order to prevent "brain damage" allegedly consequent upon neglect.

In response, we produced a critique of the neuroscientific strand of "A Child's Timeframe"; it was made available to the judiciary and was published on-line (White and Wastell, 2013) so that it could be read and cited by lawyers if they so wished. This underscores the fact that "evidence" is being mobilized by all sides of this debate to support preferred moral positions on the relative merits of "child centred" versus "whole family" paradigms, and on the case for and nature of state intervention in family life. The evidence must be spoken for and there are a number of ways in which it can be presented.

In this response we drew upon the original journal science, and set it against the handbook version which we contended had informed "A Child's Timeframe", leading it to present the knowledge base as fixed and settled. Our principal argument was that these decisions regarding inclusion and exclusion had had a profound effect on the neuroscientific strand of the report. "A Child's Timeframe", we contended, had relied heavily on synthesized secondary sources, such as the Harvard Center, and non-peer-reviewed textbooks. Thus, it had presented as certain a field in which knowledge was far from settled and not "policy ready". In fact, Brown and

Ward did begin in just this place, citing recent thorough reviews of the emergent knowledge on the neuroscience of parenting by Belsky and de Haan (2011), and another by McCrory *et al.* (2012). Slightly expanding the actual quotation used by Brown and Ward, Belsky and de Haan argue that although the brain "packs a punch" for policy makers, "the study of parenting and brain development is not even yet in its infancy; it would be more appropriate to conclude that it is still in the embryonic stage" (Belsky and de Haan, 2011: 409–410).

After beginning their review with appropriate caution, the knowledge base is thereafter described as though it delivered certainty about the damage caused to the brain by neglectful parenting. This, as we have seen, is a strong motif in the popular mind-set. The nature of the neuroscientific claims in "A Child's Timeframe" made our counter-argument relatively straightforward to construct from within the neuroscientific discourse itself. Much of the primary work is on animals and, even here, findings have often proved difficult to replicate. This is willingly acknowledged by the primary scientists. The work on humans has largely come from extreme clinical populations, most notably children raised in orphanages in Romania, Russia and sometimes China (supplemented by a small number of post-mortem studies, and cohort studies, of abused children or adults with psychiatric or psychological symptomatology). These studies yield important understandings of the effect of extreme institutional abuse, and thankfully much promising evidence of plasticity and resilience (Wastell and White, 2012). However, we argued, they cannot be used as though they have predictive validity for anything other than a tiny and extreme minority of the UK population of poorly parented children. Nevertheless, this is precisely how these studies were being used by certain child welfare campaigners from North America; this is also reflected in their use by Brown and Ward. To support our argument that the case was over-stated we used a number of examples from the report. For example, a graph reproduced with permission of the Center on the Developing Child at Harvard University, which appears to show "sensitive periods" for the development of a range of abilities, does not have a "y" (vertical) axis, and appears to show that a child's critical period for language acquisition is about 7 months of age. The figure suggests that the window is all but slammed shut by the age of 1 year when the child may, of course, have lots of receptive language, but is unlikely actually to be able to speak. Higher cognitive functions are shown as peaking at the age of 2. The "graph" is, in fact, a visual aid packaged to persuade.

To understand how the complex and often contradictory evidence from neuroscience had come to be assembled with such confidence in "A Child's Timeframe" we must look at the conditions of its production. As Ward and Brown note in their response to our critique, their original report had been:

> overseen by a steering group, and was then peer-reviewed by three independent academics, all of professorial status and each with expertise in a relevant field (early years, law and neuroscience). The report benefitted from their suggestions for change and improvement. Neither the referees nor the steering group

criticised our approach, which they regarded as both balanced and consistent with current evidence (Ward and Brown, 2013: 1181–1182).

They state (p. 1182) that they were "not commissioned to present 'contradictory' or 'controversial' evidence, rather to produce the best possible account of the accepted consensus currently within the field". Furthermore, they clarify that they were asked to produce a simplified guide to the knowledge base, and indeed had been asked by the steering group to simplify the arguments in a previous draft still further. There had been, therefore, a specific instruction in the brief to engage in "pragmatic reductionism" for the purposes of clarity. They end their response with a suggestion that our critique would undermine the case for more timely intervention to protect children from the effects of abuse and result in further harm to their well-being.

"A Child's Timeframe" had thus been commissioned explicitly to simplify and demystify journal science. In this it had succeeded. None of the specific arguments we had made about the impossibility of predicting the degree or likelihood of damage in an asymptomatic infant were addressed in Brown and Ward's rejoinder. It was not necessary for anyone to do so, since the neuroscience so assembled seemed to show what everybody already knew, sitting common-sensically alongside other aspects of the developmentalist narrative. Neuroscience thus buttresses an older argument about the role of the state in family life, old wine in new bottles. But the seductive new "certainties" deflect moral and ethical questions from their proper context, and render sensible debate a somewhat risky business. That was our underlying concern.

The real problem with the policy leap from orphanage to housing estate, is that we do not have any reliable understanding of the "dose" of neglect required to produce a given degree of "damage". More fundamentally, what do brains actually add to the argument? Either we can see the damage behaviourally or physically, and thus do not need the brain to make our moral arguments, or we cannot. If we cannot see the damage, current knowledge does not provide the grounds for inferring it into being. Conversely, if the brain were normal, does this mean the child should stay in adverse circumstances? We may have very good reasons to feel an infant should not stay with their family, but we must make those arguments on the basis of manifest evidence. Is the idea of a miserable life in need of a brain image to make us take it seriously?

Conclusion

[Propaganda works by] giving modern man all-embracing, simple explanations without which he could not live. Man is doubly reassured by propaganda: first, because it tells him all the reasons behind the developments which unfold, and second because it provides a solution for all the problems which arise, which otherwise would seem insoluble (Ellul, 1965: 147).

Societies hold aspirations for the betterment of their citizens, many of the projects so spawned focus on the very young. Concentrating resources on poor parenting, rather than poverty itself is a noteworthy contemporary twist. The early invention machinery is held in place by a neuro-fascination behind which well-meaning campaigners gather. There are problems with this, however. First, the neuroscience does not say what they say it says and second, once the genie is out of the bottle the notion of damaged infant brains creates the conditions for one of the state's most draconian interventions – the compulsory removal of children on the precautionary principle. To quote from a distinguished neuroscience professor commenting on this matter in the *Guardian*[4] newspaper in 2016:

> Zoe Williams [journalist] is rightly critical of the scary image of the shrivelled brain reproduced from the cover of MP Graham Allen's report to the government on the importance of the first three years of a child's life, for it makes a travesty of what neuroscience can and cannot say about early child development. The image derives from a short unrefereed report at a US neuroscience meeting, without information as to its provenance other than that it is from a three year old abused child. That children's brains and their synaptic connections develop rapidly in early years is well established. That young children benefit from a stable, loving and secure environment is … common sense. But there really is no good evidence that these two statements are related. That is indeed a bridge too far (Steven Rose, Emeritus Professor of Neuroscience, The Open University).

Propaganda must be challenged. It is time to stop and think, time to break out of the brain seduction.

Notes

1 https://www.gov.uk/government/speeches/prime-ministers-speech-on-life-chances,   last accessed 30/07/16.
2 Data taken from https://welfarestatefutures.org/research-network/facsk-family-complexity-and-social-work-a-comparative-study-of-family-based-welfare-work-in-different-welfare-regimes/.
3 Re N (Children) (Adoption: Jurisdiction) [2015] EWCA Civ 1112, para. 16.
4 http://www.theguardian.com/society/2014/apr/29/early-years-interventions-social-justice.

References

Allen, G. (2011a). *Early intervention: Next steps*. London: Department for Work and Pensions and Cabinet Office.
Allen, G. (2011b). *Early intervention: Smart investment, massive savings*. London: Department for Work and Pensions and Cabinet Office.
Allen, G. and Smith, I. D. (2009). *Early intervention: Good parents, great kids, better citizens*. London: Centre for Social Justice and the Smith Institute.
Belsky, J. and de Haan, M. (2011). Parenting and children's brain development: The end of the beginning. *Journal of Child Psychology and Psychiatry*, 52(4): 409–428.
Broadhurst, K., Alrouch, B., Yeend, E., Harwin, J., Shaw, M., Pilling, M., Mason, C. and Kershaw, S. (2015a). Connecting events in time to identify a hidden population: Birth

mothers and their children in recurrent care proceedings in England. *British Journal of Social Work*, 45(8): 2241–2260. doi:10.1093/bjsw/bcv130

Broadhurst, K., Shaw, M., Kershaw, S., Harwin, J., Alrouh, B., Mason., C. and Pilling, M. (2015b). Vulnerable birth mothers and repeat losses of infants to public care: Is targeted reproductive health care ethically defensible? *Journal of Social Welfare and Family Law*, 37(1), 84–98. doi:10.1080/09649069.2015.998007

Broer, T. and Pickersgill, M. (2015). (Low) expectations, legitimization, and the contingent uses of scientific knowledge: Engagements with neuroscience in Scottish social policy and services. *Engaging Science, Technology, and Society*, 1: 47–66.

Brown, R. and Ward, H. (2013). Decision-making within the child's timeframe. Working Paper No. 16. Loughborough, UK: Childhood Wellbeing Research Centre, Loughborough University.

Bruer, J. T. (1999). *The myth of the first three years*. New York: The Free Press.

Dawson, G., Hessl, D. and Frey, K. (1994). Social influences on early developing biological and behavioural systems related to risk for affective disorder. *Development and Psychopathology*, 6(4): 759–779.

Edwards, R., Gillies, V. and Horsley, N. (2015). Brain science and early years policy: Hopeful ethos or "cruel optimism"? *Critical Social Policy*, 35(2): 167–187.

Ellul, J. (1965). *Propaganda: The formation of men's attitudes*. New York: Vintage Books.

Farmer, R. L. (2009). *Neuroscience and social work practice: The missing link*. Thousand Oaks, CA: Sage.

Featherstone, B., White, S. and Morris, K. (2014). *Re-imagining child protection: Towards humane social work with families*. Bristol, UK: Policy Press, University of Bristol.

Fenton Glynn, C. (2015). *Adoption without consent*. Brussels: Policy Department C: Citizens' Rights and Constitutional Affairs, European Parliament.

Field, F. (2010). The foundation years: Preventing poor children becoming poor adults. The report of the Independent Review on Poverty and Life Chances, HM Government. http://webarchive.nationalarchives.gov.uk/20110120090128/http://povertyreview.independent.gov.uk/media/20254/poverty-report.pdf.

Greenhalgh, T. and Russell, J. (2006). Reframing evidence synthesis as rhetorical action in the policy making drama. *Healthcare Policy*, 1(2): 34–42.

Huntsinger, E. T. and Luecken, L. J. (2004). Attachment relationships and health behavior: The mediational role of self-esteem. *Psychology & Health*, 19(4): 515–526.

Lloyd-Jones, E. (2013). Decision making within a child's timescale: Who decides? *Family Law*, 43(8): 1053–1055.

McCrory, E., De Brito, S. and Viding, E. (2012). The link between child abuse and psychopathology: A review of neurobiological and genetic research. *Journal of the Royal Society of Medicine*, 105(4): 151–156.

McWilliams, L. A. and Bailey, S. J. (2010). Associations between adult attachment ratings and health conditions: Evidence from the National Comorbidity Survey Replication. *Health Psychology*, 29(4): 446–453.

Perry, B. D. (2002). Childhood experience and the expression of genetic potential: What childhood neglect tells us about nature and nurture. *Brain and Mind*, 3(1): 79–100.

Rose, N. (2010). Screen and intervene: Governing risk brains. *History of the Human Sciences*, 23(1): 79–105.

Shonkoff, J. P. and Bales, S. (2011). Science does not speak for itself: Translating child development research for the public and its policymakers. *Child Development*, 82(1): 17–32.

Stevens, A. (2011). Telling policy stories: An ethnographic study of the use of evidence in policy-making in the UK. *Journal of Social Policy*, 40(2): 237–255.

Ward, H. and Brown, R. (2013). Decision-making within a child's timeframe: A response. *Family Law Journal*, 43: 1181–1186.

Wastell, D. and White, S. (2012). Blinded by neuroscience: Social policy and the myth of the infant brain. *Families, Relationships and Societies: An International Journal of Research and Debate*, 1(3): 397–414.

Wastell, D. and White, S. (2017). *Blinded by science: Social implications of epigenetics, biology and genetics*. Bristol, UK: Policy Press, University of Bristol.

White, S. and Wastell, D. G. (2013). Response to Brown and Ward "Decision-Making within the Child's Timeframe". http://dx.doi.org/10.2139/ssrn.2325357.

White, S. and Wastell, D. G. (2016). The rise and rise of prevention science in UK family welfare: Surveillance gets under the skin. *Families, Relationships and Societies*. https://doi.org/10.1332/204674315X14479283041843.

4

ANYTHING TO DIVERT ATTENTION FROM POVERTY

Helen Penn

Introduction

This chapter examines how interpretations of neuroscientific ideas in early childhood have been used by international organizations to promote a particular view of international development. Like other misinterpretations of neuroscience discussed in this book, it has resulted in an instrumental approach which simplifies the complex business of bringing up children, and limits the understanding of childhood, in a complex, unequal and tension filled world. The idea of early intervention, that is, stimulation programmes for infants to "develop their brains", has been adopted and powerfully pushed by worldwide international organizations concerned about children and their future – UNICEF, WHO, the World Bank and many others. Early intervention, it has been argued, is an important route to combating global poverty. Global poverty is shocking; so for that matter is all chronic poverty and inequality. But why should early intervention be any kind of panacea? What has led the international ECD/ECEC community to champion its cause?

I do not wish to deny the good intentions and concerns about poverty held by proponents of early intervention. Poverty is very real and corrosive, and any attempts to address it are worthy. But I would argue, good intentions are not enough. A more thorough analysis of the implicit as well as explicit assumptions and predictions of the "brain science" which is said to underpin early intervention programmes is needed. So is an understanding of the wider political, economic and social contexts of young children's lives in the situation where any intervention is being carried out (Boyden *et al.*, 2015).

In the chapter I first discuss the nature of global poverty (not an easy task in a few paragraphs!) and its impact on children. The limitations of "brain science" have been widely discussed, and I briefly cite some of its critics. It is a starting point for this book that extrapolations from neuroscientific findings often are deeply flawed.

Here I focus, in particular, on how "brain science" is being used to support particular programmes and assumptions in developing countries. I argue that its usage derives from socio-economic liberalism, and that it reflects a kind of cultural hegemony that verges on racism. I also argue that "brain science" has in practice in this context led to a devaluation of women as mothers and carers. Finally, I explore the options for intervention in early childhood that might be – and are being – pursued as an alternative to those based on "brain science".

Global poverty

It is conservatively estimated 60 percent of the world's children live in poverty. The extent of poverty – and the extent of inequality and its variations – are statistically difficult to chart (Milanovic, 2016). But it is beyond doubt that chronic poverty exists and that its effects are devastating (Hulme, 2016; Boyden and Bourdillon, 2012). The poorest children and their families do not routinely have access to the goods and services that in rich countries are assumed to be necessary for well-being – adequate food, shelter, access to water, sanitation, clothing, shoes, fuel, safe transport, health services and medicine, education and most household goods (let alone digital media). *Every day* an estimated 19,000 children under 5 die: *one unnecessary child death every five seconds all day every day* (Hulme, 2016: 2). This is an extraordinary cull of the child population and one that everyone should deeply regret.

There has been a slight decrease in world poverty rates in the last 25 years. This depends on how poverty is measured, and measurement rates have themselves varied (Milanovic, 2016; Pogge and Sengupta, 2015). However, it seems clear that in most countries, rich and poor alike, over the last 10 to 20 years, the income gap between the richest and poorest families has increased. The rich have got richer, so that globally the wealth of 1 percent of the population equals that of the poorest 40 percent. The continuance of chronic enduring poverty in poor and middle income countries, and the concomitant growth of inequality, is recognized as the major issue for international development (Collier, 2007; Chang, 2008; Milanovic, 2016). Stiglitz (2012) argues that inequality on this scale demonstrably leads to an impoverished understanding of democracy, as rich elites use their position to shape policy in rich and poor countries alike.

The new UN Sustainable Development Goals (SDGs), which replace the barely successful UN Millennium Development goals, are, in the words of one influential commentator, *grotesquely unambitious* (Pogge and Sengupta, 2015). Most actions to address chronic poverty in low and middle income countries have been minor and ameliorative, and they have frequently failed because they require fundamental global scale economic reform (Deaton, 2013; Nicolai *et al.*, 2015).

There have been many recent books addressing global poverty and the function of international aid. There is also a considerable debate about the ethics of the dealings between rich and poor countries, most notably by Singer (2010) and Illingworth *et al.* (2011). These views are ably summed up by Hulme (2016). He highlights the complexity of global relations in the phrase "Context is King" – situations differ from country to country, and within countries; past history, and the very terrain, shape what is possible; and at the same time there is damaging global economy which it is almost impossible to track or regulate.

But even allowing for very difficult and varying situations, and the problems of monitoring or curtailing international money flows, there are some solutions, on a country level, which seem to be more promising than others. Unconditional cash transfers, i.e. a basic guaranteed income for the poorest, is becoming an increasingly widespread and successful strategy in dealing with chronic poverty (Ferguson, 2015). Clamping down on tax havens and improving international trade agreements is a way in which the international community could better enable poor countries to control their own budgets. Refusing to export arms would dramatically alter trade balances. Limiting the influence of international and philanthropic organizations who seek to promote aid as a technical solution to well defined problems, and who promote their own organizational interests in the process, would make for more realistic and context sensitive programmes. It is generally regarded as extremely difficult – politically and practically – to make structural changes and bring about the massive redistribution, curbs on consumption in rich countries, environmental regulation and open migration that would significantly change the lives of the poor (Buxton and Hayes, 2015; Kwon and Kim, 2014).

The fans of "brain science"

The complexities of understanding and addressing global poverty in low and middle income countries is a major issue, and it affects the future of rich countries as well as poorer ones (Stiglitz, 2012; Hulme, 2016). But in the niche world of early child development (ECD)/ early childhood education and care (ECEC), many see brain stimulation of infants as a main route to combat poverty. The argument put forward by major agencies such as the World Bank (Young and Mustard, 2008), WHO (Maggi et al., 2005) and UNICEF, and a host of smaller agencies, is briefly as follows: If the growth of an infant's neural network in the brain is encouraged through "stimulation", both physiological (nutrient supplements) and intellectual, the child will grow up to become a more productive citizen, and thereby better able to contribute to the future prosperity of his nation. This proposition has been expressed in a variety of overlapping documents, and published in journals as prestigious as *The Lancet* (Grantham-McGregor et al., 2007; Engle et al., 2011; Chan, 2013) and *The Economist* (2014). For example, a recent UNICEF publication (2014) titled *Building Better Brains: New Frontiers in Early Child Development* claims that acting on the findings of neuroscience will have "significant implications for the future of millions of the world's most disadvantaged children and their societies" (2014: 1). (The caption for the accompanying frontispiece cartoon to the UNICEF document is "The Three Pound Universe", a reference to the weight of the brain!)

Neuroscientific findings, at a first casual reading, seem to suggest that there is a hard scientific basis to the idea that early intervention is most likely to be successful.

Helping the child's brain to grow through stimulation is why early intervention works. One of the most widely cited contributors in this arena is a retired Canadian haematologist, Fraser Mustard. His work is published and recycled by some of the most eminent of USA based think tanks, including the Brookings Institute and the World Bank; and the Canadian McCain Foundation actively promotes his work. His contribution is summarized in a rambling paper for the Brookings Institute called *Early Child Development and Experience-based Brain Development – The Scientific Underpinnings of the Importance of Early Child Development in a Globalized World* (Mustard, 2006).

Fraser Mustard had little doubt that a solution is on hand for the most intractable of problems.

> To achieve the goal of enhancing the competence and quality of our populations, and establish sustainable, stable, equitable, tolerant, pluralistic, democratic societies, we have to find ways to optimize human development, health, and well-being in all regions of the world. The continuing evolution and improved function of our brain will influence how well we cope with the challenges and opportunities we face today.
>
> To do this we have to understand the development of the brain and its continuing evolution and how experience in early life affects its development (2006: 47).

And since low income countries cannot – for reasons that are not spelled out – provide early intervention programmes on their own, international agencies must step in.

> Societies in the developing world will not be able to make the investments to ensure good early child development unless international agencies such as the World Bank, the United Nations and other international organizations provide more support and leadership. One needs to ask the question within these international agencies, "Why is there such a gap between what we know and what we do?" If we do not close this gap, there is a high risk that given the conditions of today's world, there will be a substantial failure to improve the competence and well-being of populations and improve equity, that could put our societies and experiments in civilization at risk (2006: 47).

In 2016 the OECD development group hosted an international conference in Paris which showcased the work of those philanthropic agencies, such as the McCain Foundation, promoting ideas like those of Fraser Mustard, as a means of addressing poverty in low income countries (Edu Ensemble, 2016).

This rhetoric, whilst carrying a veneer of equality and concern, is profoundly depressing in its failure to acknowledge real, extremely complex, problems of chronic poverty and inequality within and between nations. Instead, brain stimulation of young children is put forward as a route to a better future for individual families. The analogy that is used, especially by those concerned with the health and welfare of young children, is that just as the growing body benefits from a wide range of micro-nutrients, so the growing brain needs external stimulation. For the most part these early intervention programmes are targeted at "the first 1000 days" of a child's life. But in addition they are considered as a viable and cost effective alternative to more comprehensive service provision, which is regarded by donors as unaffordable in low income countries.

The claims for the efficacy of these early intervention programmes in developing countries have been extensive, but they are coming under increasing scrutiny, from a variety of sources. For instance, the organization 3ie, which specializes in systematic reviews and evidence based findings in developing countries, is increasingly critical of the evidence provided, since like is rarely compared with like, and context is frequently ignored (Leroy et al., 2013; White, 2013).

"Brain science" – Does it exist?

Claims to understand the processes of neural development, and consequently, for the efficacy of early intervention, are grossly overstated. Bruer (1999), in particular, has shown how relatively insignificant findings from neuroscience have been blown up out of all proportion as they are applied in the field of early child development. Rutter and Solantaus (2014) call this process *Translation gone awry*. The neuroscientific findings about the development of young children's brains may contribute to highly specialized neuroscientific debates about the architecture of the brain, or about the methodologies and equipment used to analyse brain functioning, but as Rutter and others argue, the translation is the problem – highly specialized and highly limited findings *cannot* be extrapolated to make general prescriptions about social policy.

Most neuroscientists point to the extraordinary complexity of the brain and its linked bodily systems. We have only rudimentary knowledge about the brain's functioning within the even more complex phenomenon that is the body. The brain cannot be considered apart from the rest of the bodily functions – to take a crude example, the development of the brain is closely linked to the neuronal and hormonal development of the gut in ways which are minimally understood. Our limited knowledge of the brain as a physical organism *cannot* be extrapolated to present a picture of a thinking, feeling human being. Yet these limits to our current understanding are routinely ignored by the early childhood lobby. The schematic picture, widely available on the web, with the image of a brain next to a stack of gold summarizes the evils that early intervention can avoid through brain stimulation!

A report from the McCain Foundation includes a diagram of the brain with the caption: *The Brain as the Foundation of the Human Mind*. In this diagram, an executive "mind" mapped onto the brain allocates functions to "create, reflect, respond, dream, love, express, wonder, purpose, do, learn act", etc. (McCain et al., 2011: 53). No self-respecting neuroscientist would ever make such claims.

Socio-economic individualism

One of the attractions of "brain science" is its apparent endorsement of Heckman's ideas about early intervention (e.g. Heckman and Masterov, 2005). James Heckman, the Nobel prize winning economist, has long argued that if some kind of remedial action is to be taken for dysfunctional and disruptive children, it is most effective when children are young. His work, originally based on an analysis of three long-term randomized controlled trials of early interventions (in themselves problematic – see Penn *et al.*, 2006), is located within a particular theoretical stance on family functioning and its economic consequences. As a shorthand, I call this human capital theory.

Originally the idea of human capital, put forward by Sen (2001) in his book *Development as Freedom,* stressed the societal conditions – primarily, universal health and education – necessary in order to enable human beings – especially the poor – to thrive. Free from the most pressing anxieties of poverty, and with basic services in place, people would be able to develop their potential. However, this humane human capital approach has now been superseded by a more neo-liberal approach, which holds that individual humans are responsible for their own development and prosperity, and for nurturing their own futures, and structural inequalities are relatively unimportant. Individuals and families have to take the situation as they find it. They must equip themselves to cope and prosper in the modern "globalized" world, to get on and be successful and competitive.

In this scenario, the family – rather than structural change or the provision of services – is the locus for improvement. Heckman and Gary Becker (another Nobel prize winner) have based their economic predictions on a particular analysis of family functioning (Becker, 1993). In this reckoning the poor are principally responsible for their own shortcomings, and can be taught to perform better. The family is the major producer of those skills which are indispensable for students and workers. Unfortunately, many families have failed to perform this task well. This retards the growth of the quality of the workforce. Dysfunctional families are also a major determinant of child participation in crime and other costly pathological behaviour. On productivity grounds alone it appears to make sound sense to invest in young children from disadvantaged environments.

In this analysis the family, and especially the mother, is responsible for inculcating in her children the necessary skills and attitudes to cope within a competitive environment and become prosperous in the long term. All other mechanisms and props for individual human development are regarded as minor in comparison to the fundamental role of the individual family. Many children are disadvantaged, because their mothers fail to create the right sort of environment to help their children develop the right skills and attitudes. In these cases, to prevent further havoc, the state may need to intervene. If the state does intervene, such intervention is likely to be most effective when children are young.

Heckman's argument that early learning and early experiences are a powerful tool on the road to success and prosperity has made him a hero in the early childhood community, despite other, more disturbing aspects of his theoretical perspectives on society. For example, like Becker, he takes inequality for granted, and is only concerned about targeting the least successful; inequality can be reduced by better equipping the poorest children to cope better, through early educational intervention; less needy parents can purchase the services they need in the private market.

Heckman does not argue, as for example the OECD has done, that equitable access to early years services per se is likely to reduce inequality. His argument is that the efficacy of interventions with the poorest families have been proved through long term randomized controlled trials (Perry High Scope, Abecdarian, Chicago child centres – see Penn *et al.*, 2006). As an economist the exact nature of the educational intervention is outside of his remit, but his stance assumes that expert, technical educators exist, who can diagnose poor learning and put it right. In his view proven expertise exists to run early intervention programmes, and measure the outcomes of any intervention.

Many in the early childhood community have assumed that Heckman's ideas are underpinned by neuroscience. Early intervention appears to be confirmed by ideas about the rapid growth of the brain in the first few years of life. The reason why intervention is effective is apparently because the brain is most flexible and malleable, and is busy forming the synaptic connections which are the basis of learning, when children are very young. Heckman and neuroscience have been seamlessly connected. Many agencies have adopted the slogan *the first 1000 days* as a shortcut guide in formulating early intervention programmes.

Cultural hegemony/racism

But arguments about brain science and brain stimulation are not new, especially in low income countries. They have a surprisingly long history.

> The Black child has no toys. He does not find around him any occasion to arouse his intellect ... the early childhood of the Black always takes place in an environment intellectually *inferior* to *any imaginable in Europe.* ... The Black child remains inactive for long hours. He thus undergoes a terrifying head shrinking from which it is virtually impossible to recover. The neural centres of his cortex, which should normally be used for exercise, do not receive the necessary stimuli for their development (Maistriaux, 1955: 88).

This quotation is 60 years old, although in content not so very different from contemporary accounts about brain shrinkage and the need for stimulation. It is taken from a French colonial text published in 1955. There are many such colonial/religious references to the stunted brains of Africans, an ideology reaching its apogee in apartheid South Africa. It has been a major sign of progress that no serious contemporary analyst would now make comments based on skin colour or racial origin. But it is possible to argue that poverty and low income have replaced race as a marker of inadequacy, and poverty is a signal that intervention is necessary, as race once was.

The central idea contained in the colonial extract is that the environment in which poor children in low income countries grow up is intellectually inferior. This idea of a lack or a deficit, in comparison with (middle class) Euro-American standards of childrearing, is implicit in much of the work on early intervention promoted by international agencies. Most of the research on early intervention derives from low income families in the USA. Their situation is assumed to be similar to that of children in low income countries more generally. For instance, a major review of early stimulation programmes carried out by Baker-Henningham and Lopez Boo (2010) for the InterAmerican Development Bank makes *no distinction at all* between the circumstances of very poor children in the USA and those in low income countries as different as Peru, South Africa, Jamaica and the Philippines. The assumption of those advocating early intervention is that the brain is an organ that develops (or doesn't develop) in the same way for all children, and therefore the same general prescription for early stimulation applies equally:

> The evidence cited in this report indicates that early stimulation interventions are effective in improving child and maternal outcomes and these benefits are likely to be sustained over the long term. Interventions should target younger and more disadvantaged children and their families and should involve active involvement of the children's caregivers. Interventions should also promote the well-being of families as a whole, particularly the mothers. Interventions of higher quality, greater intensity and of longer duration are likely to be the most effective (2010: 62).

These "scientifically based" prescriptions inform the work of agencies providing early childhood development programmes in low income countries. They include standard Western play based interventions for societies where play is differently understood and rarely adult initiated, and activities such as shared reading with young children in poor communities where household books are unknown or unavailable and illiteracy rates are high!

Any indigenous ideas or assumptions about childrearing – for example about child-to-child activities, or about the participation of children in the work life of their families, or about multi-lingualism, or about dance or art as means of expression, or about spiritual well-being – all the many facets of cultural diversity and richness are simply ignored. Instead the interventions are mostly low cost and home based, and are crude in their assumptions about the nature of stimulation or about the material possessions families are likely to have.

The absence of awareness of any cultural differences or circumstances between the poor of the USA and those of any other country is astonishing, given the substantial body of work in cultural anthropology. Leaving aside any political analysis of poverty, many researchers in early childhood have tried to draw attention to the importance of cultural beliefs and values (Nsamenang, 2008; Penn, 2012).

Distinguished researchers such as Bruner (2000), Gottleib (2004), LeVine (2003), Serpell and Adamson-Holley (2015) and Correa-Chavez and others (2015) have all detailed the values and cultural approaches that shape young children's learning, the multiplicity of ways young children learn, and the tools that shape their learning. These authors stress the importance of local contexts and understandings in childrearing. Yet this literature is rarely referred to. It is the pervasiveness of crude ideas about brain stimulation that have partly enabled agencies to ignore or gloss over cultural difference.

LeVine summarized one of the key cultural aspects of difference like this:

> Compared with Africans, American infants experience a particularly sharp distinction between situations in which they are alone and those in which they are with others – for African infants are never alone and are often present as non-participants in situations dominated by adult interaction, whilst the American infant is often kept in solitary confinement when he is not the centre of adult attention. This creates (for the American) a bifurcation between the extremes of isolation and inter-personal excitement that is unknown in Africa and may underlie some of the striking differences in interactive style between peoples of the two continents (2003: 82).

Poverty in low income countries tends to be regarded as an undifferentiated condition, as race once was; a condition which is best ameliorated or offset by the "scientific" intervention of Euro/American trained experts, who are informed about how best to promote brain stimulation through early intervention, and who work through international and multi-lateral aid agencies.

Ignoring women

Early intervention programmes in low income countries have tended to focus on various kinds of home visiting, in order to teach mothers how to stimulate their children and "grow their brains". Most of the programmes reviewed in *The Lancet* (above), for example, fall into this category. Such programmes have the advantage of being very cheap, compared with any kind of service provision, and very unchallenging and unproblematic, compared with any form of political action. But such programmes make untested assumptions about the availability and willingness of mother/carers to participate, a matter of some concern (Samman *et al.*, 2016). As well as the instrumental view of children being acted upon in order to manipulate their development (which in itself is ethically problematic – Morrow, 2013), a striking aspect of the research on early intervention is the absolute lack of voice of those mothers/families who are being targeted. It is possible to argue that such studies are discriminatory against women. Economistic/neuroscientific approaches which do not acknowledge the contribution of women through unpaid caring work, or indeed recognize the burdens poor women face, are unlikely to make much of a difference and, indeed, hinder proper analysis (Bakker and Silvey, 2008; Razavi, 2011).

Mothers and carers may overtly co-operate but tacitly show their dislike of the programmes by simply not turning up. Very few early intervention projects report on participation rates. Yet there are some indications to suggest that the participation rates of mothers, carers and home visitors in these early intervention programmes are much more erratic than generally admitted (Penn, 2015). Even in the much cited Perry High Scope longitudinal cost-benefit early intervention programme, the home visitors (an integral part of the programme) were almost all unable to complete their regular schedule of visits (Penn et al., 2006).

Women's caring responsibilities and how they impact on their lives and those of their children affects poor women more than wealthier professional women. Women with reasonable incomes can rely on servants and other forms of domestic help. Women domestics, by contrast, often tend to be internal or external migrants – who may even find themselves neglecting or abandoning their own children in order to earn a living looking after other women's children (Heymann, 2003, 2006; Hochschild and Ehrenreich, 2003; Razavi, 2011). Recent work by Samman et al. (2016) suggests that women have suffered particularly from internal rural-urban migration within poor countries, and can be described as "the new poor". Women, often on their own with disrupted family networks and burdensome jobs in the informal sector (as domestic servants, or market traders or in menial jobs), struggle to provide for their children. In these circumstances, Samman et al. (2016) suggest that an estimated *35 million young children worldwide* are left alone or cared for by siblings, in dangerous situations in shanty towns or unsafe areas, whilst their mothers work. UN Women (2016) have also highlighted the need to take carers into account in any intervention programmes.

Because there is little investment in ECEC services in low income countries, most childcare provision, by default, tends to be privately provided. But the private sector is very variable. In low income countries, at the top-end, provision mirrors the best of Euro-American standards, and is very costly for parents. At the bottom end, provision tends to be of very poor quality by any conceivable standards. Mothers pay for what they can afford, and a private market system thus exacerbates inequality. The poorest provision is in the poorest areas and serves the poorest children and vice versa (Woodhead and Streuli, 2013; Penn and Maynard, 2010).

Conclusion

People are justifiably concerned over the impact of poverty on children's lives, especially in low income countries, and want to do something about it. But efficacy of interventions depends on careful analysis of the problems and evaluation of the efforts made to resolve them. The argument put forward here is that the idea of brain stimulation is a distracting and misleading short cut to understanding of poverty.

Even if one were to focus just on young children and the micro-interventions which might be possible, the current focus on early intervention is misleading.

DfID (Department for International Development, UK) has been supporting a model research programme, called *Young Lives*. This is a 15 year longitudinal project, involving 12,000 children in four countries – Ethiopia, Vietnam, Andhra Pradesh (a large region of India) and Peru. The project mapped the progress of children, using quantitative and qualitative data – including interviews with the children and their families. As the authors conclude:

> The problem with "investing in children" as a means of realising economic growth is that children do not constitute a homogeneous group in terms of potential human capital. Children have differing skills and capacities and contribute to societies in differing ways, not always measurable in economic terms. Human-capital models offer a powerful, politically persuasive framework for policy development, but they must be understood as additional to, and not alternative to, more fundamental principles of social justice (Boyden *et al.*, 2015: 34).

One of the striking aspects of international development is how fast old ideas are jettisoned and new ones adopted. "Brain science" may have had its day. Much new research now focuses on the effectiveness of centred based interventions. This is partly because of the demand for such services, especially in Latin America (Institute of Fiscal Studies, 2016). 3ie have recently carried out a major systematic review of general education interventions in low income countries, and have concluded that the two policies which make the most difference to participation outcomes are school feeding programmes, and cash transfers, i.e. programmes which offer some income security and extra food security to the very poor. No other intervention was as statistically significant, and most purely educational interventions were not statistically significant at all.

The World Bank has switched from direct programme intervention to analyses of early childhood governance and structure. These reviews, known as the SABER system (Systems Approach for Better Education Results), take a systemic view of services. Each in-country review offers a comprehensive analysis of the local evidence on ECD/ECEC about levels of take-up and quality of provision. Where necessary, the World Bank researchers undertake their own research to complement official data. The SABER review makes recommendations based on this analysis, with suggestions about implementation. It pays attention to delivery mechanisms, in particular the use of the private sector.

As usual there is a danger of throwing out the baby with the bathwater. I do not wish to belittle the good intentions – and good results – of many early childhood specialists working on micro-level interventions in very difficult circumstances, and for whom brain science has been an inspiration. But in the last resort, to argue, as for example Fraser Mustard did, that "brain science" holds the key to global well-functioning is no more than an ignorant and distorted fantasy for those in denial of the world's poverty.

References

Baker-Henningham, H. and Lopez Boo, F. (2010). Early stimulation interventions in developing countries. InterAmerican Development Bank. Retrieved from www.iadb.org.

Bakker, I. and Silvey, R. (2008). *Beyond states and markets: The challenges of social reproduction.* London: Routledge.

Becker, G. (1993). *A treatise on the family.* Cambridge, MA: Harvard University Press.

Boyden, J. and Bourdillon, M. (Eds.) (2012). *Childhood poverty: Multidisciplinary approaches.* Basingstoke, UK: Palgrave Macmillan.

Boyden, J., Dircon, S. and Singh, A. (2015). Child development in a changing world: Key messages and policy gaps. Young Lives Policy Brief No. 26. Retrieved from http://www.younglives.org.uk/sites/www.younglives.org.uk/files/YL-PB26-Child%20Development%20in%20a%20Changing%20World.pdf.

Bruer, J. (1999). *The myth of the first three years.* New York: The Free Press.

Bruner, J. (2000). Foreword, in J. Delouche and A. Gottlieb (Eds.), *A world of babies: Imagined childcare guides for seven societies* (ix–xii). Cambridge, UK: Cambridge University Press.

Buxton, N. and Hayes, B. (2015). *The secure and the dispossessed: How the military and the corporations are shaping a climate-changed world.* Amsterdam: Transnational Institute.

Chan, M. (2013). Linking child survival and child development for health. *Lancet*, 381 (9877): 1514–1515.

Chang, H.-J. (2008). *Bad samaritans – Guilty secrets of rich nations and the threat to global prosperity.* London: Random House.

Collier, P. (2007). *The bottom billion.* London: Oxford University Press.

Correa-Chavez, R., Mejia-Arauziteso, R. and Rogoff, B. (2015). Children learn by observing and contributing to family and community endeavors: A cultural paradigm. *Advances in Child Development and Behaviour*, 49: 1–22.

Deaton, A. (2013). *The great escape: Health, wealth and the origins of inequality.* Princeton, NJ: Princeton University Press.

Department for International Development (DfID) (2016). Young Lives. http://www.younglives.org.uk/.

The Economist (2014). In the beginning was the word, February 22. Retrieved from http://www.economist.com/news/science-and-technology/21596923-how-babbling-babies-can-boost-their-brains-beginning-was-word.

Edu Ensemble (2016). First early childhood education action congress. Retrieved from http://eduensemble.org/?lang=en.

Engle, P. L., Fernald, L. C. H., Alderman, H., Behrman, J., O'Gara, C., Yousafzai, A., Cabral D'Mello, M., Hidrobo, M., Ulkuer, N., Ertem, I., Iltus, S. and the Global Child Development Steering Group (2011). Strategies for reducing inequalities and improving development outcomes for young children in low-income and middle-income countries. *Lancet*, 378(9799): 1339–1353.

Ferguson, J. (2015). *Give a man a fish: Reflections on the new politics of distribution North Carolina.* Durham, NC: Duke University Press.

Gottlieb, A. (2004). *The afterlife is where we come from: The culture of infancy in West Africa.* Chicago, IL: University of Chicago Press.

Grantham-McGregor, S., Cheung, Y. B., Cueto, S., Glewwe, P., Richter, L., Strupp, B. and the International Child Development Steering Group (2007). Development potential in the first five years for children in developing countries. *Lancet*, 369(9555): 60–70.

Heckman, J. and Masterov, D. (2005). The productivity argument for investing in young children. Retrieved from http://jenni.uchicago.edu/human-inequality/papers/h.

Heymann, J. (2003). *The role of ECCE in ensuring equal opportunity.* Policy Brief No. 18. Paris: UNESCO.

Heymann, J. (2006). *Forgotten families: Ending the growing crisis confronting children and working parents in the global economy.* Oxford, UK: Oxford University Press.

Hochschild, A. and Ehrenreich, B. (2003). *Global woman: Nannies, maids and sex workers in the new economy.* New York: Metropolitan Books.

Hulme, D. (2016). *Should rich nations help the poor?* Cambridge, UK: Polity Press.

Illingworth, P., Pogge, T. and Wenar, L. (2011). *Giving well: The ethics of philanthropy.* Oxford, UK: Oxford University Press.

Institute of Fiscal Studies (IFS) (2016). Conference by the Centre for the Evaluation of Development Policies focusing on evaluations of early childhood policies in Latin America. London. Papers available at https://www.ifs.org.uk/centres/EDePo/.

Kwon, H. and Kim, E. (2014). Poverty reduction and good governance: Examining the rationale of the millennium development goals. *Development and Change*, 45(2): 353–375.

Leroy, J., Gadsden, P. and Guijarro, M. (2013). *The impact of daycare programmes on child health, nutrition and development in developing countries: A systematic review.* London: International Initiative for Impact Evaluation (3ie).

LeVine, R. (2003). *Childhood socialization: Comparative studies of parenting, learning and educational change.* Hong Kong: Comparative Education Research Centre.

Maggi, S., Irwin, L., Siddiqi, A., Poureslami, I., Hertzman, E. and Hertzman, C. (2005). International perspectives on early child development: Analytic and strategic review paper. Geneva: WHO.

Maistriaux, R. (1955). La sous evolution des noirs d'Afrique. Sa nature, ses remedies. *Revue de psychologie des peoples*, 10. Cited in Erny, P. (1981) *The child and his environment in black Africa.* Translated and abridged by G. J. Wanjoh. Nairobi: Oxford University Press.

McCain, M. N., Mustard, J. F. and McCuaig, K. (2011). *Early years study 3: Making decisions, taking action.* Toronto, Canada: Margaret & Wallace McCain Family Foundation.

Milanovic, B. (2016). *Global inequality.* Cambridge, MA: Harvard University Press.

Morrow, V. (2013). Practical ethics in social research with children and families in young lives: A longitudinal study of childhood poverty in Ethiopia, Andhra Pradesh (India), Peru and Vietnam. *Methodological Innovations Online*, 8(2): 21–35.

Mustard, J. F. (2006). Early child development and experience-based brain development – The scientific underpinnings of the importance of early child development in a globalized world. Washington, DC: Brookings Institute. Retrieved from http://www.brookings.edu/views/papers/200602mustard.pdf.

Nicolai, S., Hoy, C., Berliner, T. and Aedy, T. (2015). *Projecting progress. Reaching the SDGs by 2030.* London: Development Progress.

Nsamenang, A. (2008). (Mis)Understanding ECD in Africa: The force of local and global motives, in M. Garcia, A. Pence and J. Evans (Eds.), *Africa's future, Africa's challenge.* Washington, DC: The World Bank.

Penn, H. (2012). The rhetoric and realities of early childhood programmes promoted by the World Bank in Mali, in R. Ames and A. Twum Danso Imoh (Eds.), *Childhoods at the intersection of the local and the global* (75–93). Basingstoke, UK: Palgrave Macmillan.

Penn, H. (2015). Social and political landscapes of childhood, in A. Farrell, S. L. Kagan and E. K. M. Tisdall (Eds.), *Sage handbook of early childhood research* (469–484). London: Sage.

Penn, H. and Maynard, T. (2010). *Siyabonana: Building better childhoods in South Africa.* Edinburgh, UK: Children in Scotland.

Penn, H., Burton, V., Lloyd, E., Mugford, M., Potter, S. and Sayeed, Z. (2006). *A systematic review of the economic impact of long-term centre-based early childhood interventions.* Research

Evidence in Education Library. London: Social Science Research Unit, Institute of Education. Retrieved from www.eppi.ioe.ac.uk.

Pogge, T. and Sengupta, M. (2015). The sustainable development goals: A plan for building a better world? *Journal of Global Ethics*, 11(1): 56–64.

Razavi, S. (2011). Rethinking care in a development context. *Development and Change*, 42(4): 873–904.

Rutter, M. and Solantaus, T. (2014). Translation gone awry: Differences between common sense and science. *European Child & Adolescent Psychiatry*, 23(5): 247–255.

Samman, E., Presler-Marshall, E., Jones, N., with Bhatkal, T., Melamed, C., Stavropoulou, M. and Wallace, J. (2016). Women's work: Mothers, children and the global childcare crisis. Retrieved from http://www.odi.org/global-childcare-crisis.

Sen, A. (2001). *Development as freedom*. Oxford: Oxford University Press.

Serpell, R. and Adamson-Holley, D. (2015). African socialization values and nonformal educational practices: Child development, parental beliefs, and educational innovation in rural Zambia, in T. Abebe and J. Waters (Eds.), *Geographies of children and young people. Laboring and learning* (978–981). Singapore: Springer Singapore.

Singer, P. (2010). *The life you can save: How to play your part in ending world poverty*. London: Picador.

Stiglitz, J. (2012). *The price of inequality*. London: Penguin.

UNICEF (2014). Building better brains: New frontiers in early child development. Retrieved from http://www.unicef.org/earlychildhood/files/Building_better_brains____web.pdf.

UN Women (2016). Gender equality, child development and job creation. Retrieved from http://www2.unwomen.org/~/media/headquarters/attachments/sections/library/p ublications/2015/unwomen-policybrief02-genderequalitychilddevelopmentandjobcrea tion-en.pdf?v=1&d=20151216T170713.

White, H. (2013). An introduction to the use of randomized controlled trials to evaluate development interventions. *Journal of Development Effectiveness*, 5(1): 30–49.

Woodhead, M. and Streuli, N. (2013). Early education for all: Is there a role for the private sector? in P. Rebello Britto, P. Engle and C. Super (Eds.), *Handbook of early childhood development research and its impact on global policy*. Oxford, UK: Oxford University Press.

Young, M. E. and Mustard, F. (2008). Brain development and ECD: A case for investment, in M. Garcia, A. Pence and J. Evans (Eds.), *Africa's future, Africa's challenge* (71–92). Washington, DC: The World Bank.

5

THE COMPLEXITY OF TRANSLATING NEUROSCIENCE TO EDUCATION

The case of number processing

Wim Fias

Introduction

Mostly, when the societal impact of neuroscience is considered, possibilities for translation of findings to clinical therapies and educational intervention programmes are considered. Yet, as now pointed out by Vandenbroeck, the impact of neuroscience goes beyond these practical applications and extends towards a broader societal influence. Apparently, neuroscience has an attractive impact on policy makers. Probably, this is related to the intuitive conviction that being able to measure something in the brain brings us to a point where our knowledge is objective and indubitable, not needing nor deserving further discussion.

Being a cognitive neuroscientist I find this quite remarkable. It is unequivocally true that developments and advances in the neurosciences have led to previously unknown and even unimaginable possibilities to map structure and function of the living brain with methods and techniques of a fairly good reliability and validity. Hence, these technological advances allow us to meaningfully measure useful components of neural function. But, one shouldn't forget that as soon as we want to couple neural function to complex concepts like cognitive and emotional function or dysfunction, like ability and disability, like well-being, that we then have to realise that we are looking at correlates and operationalisations of these complex concepts, and not to the concepts themselves. The concepts themselves remain theoretical scientific constructs.

This has a number of important consequences, with implications to the viewpoints of Vandenbroeck. First, it means that neuroscience, as opposed to the apparent starting point of Vandenbroeck, is not a static domain of knowledge, but a dynamic scientific discipline in which theories and concepts are refined, deepened, rejected, replaced, etcetera. Hence, also in neuroscience the objective truth is an illusory myth. Second, neuroscience itself is contextualised in being subject to mechanisms of construction of truth and the effects of societal influences on it.

Instead of abstractly and systematically elaborating these ideas for the neurosciences as a whole, I prefer to provide a case study that illustrates the above ideas. I hope that the case study gives a feeling of the possibilities of a cognitive neuroscientific approach and of limitations and pitfalls, and that in doing so it demonstrates how neuroscience is a dynamic and growing domain of knowledge that is influenced by contextual factors that impact on construction of truth.

One of the domains of cognitive neuroscience where substantial progress has been made is mathematical cognition, that is the study of the neural basis of the human ability to perform mental arithmetic and to solve mathematical problems.

Mathematics is an important cognitive skill with important societal implications at several levels: school success, societal success, well-being, etcetera, all depend to some degree on mathematical skill. Early individual differences in mathematics are predictors of socioeconomic status later in life (Ritchie & Bates, 2013), making it an important issue for policy makers, teachers and practitioners, clearly with implications for early childhood care and education as well.

By matter of case study, I am going to describe how the neuroscientific study of mathematical cognition has evolved over the last two decades or so. I will illustrate how beautiful neuroscientific work led to a particular theoretical position that started to dominate the field. Speculations were made about how this theoretical position could be translated to the context of education and intervention. It absorbed an enormous amount of research resources at the cost of other theoretically fruitful positions. Importantly, this happened despite the fact that the theoretical idea is rather simple and cannot by itself do justice to the complexity of teaching mathematics and the remediation of mathematical learning disabilities.

The number sense: An important neuroscientific discovery

Understanding a number as a quantity is the most essential, most basic part of mathematical knowledge. Interestingly, the ability to enumerate is not uniquely human. Indeed, many animal species have been shown to be able to distinguish numerosities, although with varying precision.

Animals

Various species have been shown to be able to represent numerosity (i.e. the quantity of a sensory set of items; for instance, the number of objects or sounds) and to distinguish it from other numerosities. For instance, pigeons can be trained to press a certain amount of times on a lever to obtain food (Davis & Perusse, 1988). Or, fish can make a choice based on number of items (Agrillo et al., 2007). Interestingly, this ability follows a specific pattern: with increasing numerical distance, the discrimination between two collections becomes easier. And with increasing set size, a larger distance is needed to allow accurate discrimination. This ratio-dependent discrimination indicates that the number representations are increasingly less precise with increasing number. Although representational accuracy may differ, the ratio-dependent ability to discriminate number has been demonstrated in almost every species that was tested. This suggests that number is an essential and basic sensory feature and that the availability of *a number sense* that allows the effortless extraction of this sensory information has an evolutionary advantage explaining why it is widespread across species.

Interestingly, single cell recording studies in macaque monkeys – single cell recording allows the measuring of the electrophysiological response of individual neurons to specific stimuli – have demonstrated the existence of number-selective neurons in specific regions of the monkey brain (Nieder & Miller, 2004). More specifically the intraparietal sulcus (a specific and clearly identifiable sulcus in parietal cortex) and the prefrontal cortex host neurons that are tuned to a specific numerosity. Some neurons respond preferentially if one object is shown, other neurons if two objects are shown, etc. The characteristics of these neurons are perfectly in line with the behavioural regularities: the tuning of the neurons becomes more imprecise with increasing number, explaining the effect of distance and set size. This correspondence between behavioural and neural characteristics suggests that these neurons constitute the neural basis of the number sense (in the literature also called the approximate number system).

Infants

Developmental studies in humans have shown that infants, even newborns of a few hours old, are able to distinguish numerosities, again in a ratio-dependent way (Izard et al., 2009). With brain imaging methods ratio-dependent neural responses have been observed in the intraparietal sulcus. With electroencephalography (EEG, which measures the electrophysiological aspects of neural activity by means of electrodes positioned on the scalp) in children as young as 6 months of age (Hyde & Spelke, 2011), and with functional magnetic resonance imaging (fMRI, that measures local metabolic energy consumption in the brain by means of an MR scanner) at 4 years of age (Cantlon et al., 2006). The behavioural and neural similarity of the sensitivity to number between animals and human infants suggests that the number sense is shared between human infants and animals of different species and can thus be considered an evolutionary developed and phylogenetically old system.

Adults

Ontogenetic development doesn't fundamentally change this number sense system. Despite abundant experience with number through life and despite formal training of number and mathematics at school, the ability to discriminate number remains ratio-dependent, although gain can be made at the level of accuracy. Moreover, the same neural regions, with the intraparietal sulcus being the most important one, remain the core regions of the brain that process numerosity, as evidenced with EEG and fMRI (e.g. Santens *et al.*, 2010). Importantly, these regions are not only involved in the processing of quantitative information that can directly be derived from the sensory information (like number of objects or number of sounds) but are also involved when the quantitative information is expressed by symbols (e.g. Arabic notation, spoken words). Also, even though symbolic numbers refer unequivocally to specific numbers (the word six refers to exactly six elements, not five nor seven) and allow therefore in principle exact number representations, ratio-dependence remains when human adults are asked to discriminate the magnitude of symbolic numbers. This suggests that the uniquely human ability to understand and use the culturally determined symbolic number systems is built upon the biologically old number sense that allows to grasp numerosity from sensory information and that is shared with other animals.

Together, the above constitutes an internally coherent and empirically solid argument that has been construed by various disciplines (developmental psychology, neuroscience, biology) using various techniques (behavioural, computational, most advanced imaging techniques, like EEG, fMRI and other techniques that were not mentioned above, for example, fNIR). It beautifully demonstrates what advanced levels of understanding and insight can be achieved by the multidisciplinary nature of neuroscience. No wonder that many of these crucial discoveries were reported in journals of the highest impact like *Nature*, *Science* and the like.

The number sense as the foundation of mathematical skill: A nativist claim

Of course, demonstrating the existence of a number sense and describing the neurocognitive grounds of it is one thing, but on itself it doesn't show that this innate number sense constitutes the foundational basis of mathematical skill and ability. Such nativist proposals had already been made frequently, each time a new spectacular finding was reported. This happened in scientific publications as well as in popular science media (e.g. Devlin, 2005). The idea, however, became much more prevalent with the *Nature* publication that reported the results of a large scale retrospective study showing a significant correlation between the precision of the number sense at age 14 and their past math achievement scores, going back even to kindergarten (Halberda *et al.*, 2008). This correlation remained significant after controlling for performance on other cognitive tests or non-mathematical achievement measures. The fact that this study had confirmed the nativist idea that mathematical performance builds on an evolutionary old ability to distinguish non-symbolic numerosity has become a dominant idea, that has had a huge impact on basic science but also on the more applied fields of education, diagnostics and intervention.

The most influential consequence is that the level of mathematical skill that one reaches is ultimately reduced to how well one specific neurocognitive function is operating. Likewise, dyscalculia is interpreted as a homogeneous disorder that is the result of a single core deficit to the ability to approximately estimate numerosity from sensory visual input (e.g. Butterworth, 2005; Piazza *et al.*, 2010).

Accordingly, assessment tools and intervention programs have been developed. For instance, the team of Halberda has developed the Panamath. This is a simple computer-based test in which participants are presented with a cluster of blue and yellow dots on a computer screen and have to decide which of two colours has more dots. This is repeated for a series of trials and at the end, depending on the performance, a weber-fraction is computed that quantifies the precision of the number sense. This software isn't only used as a tool for scientific research, but is actively promoted as a diagnostic tool as the authors announce on their website "Ultimately, we'd like to have Panamath integrated into math curricula as an assessment tool and monitor of continued progress, as well as a fun and engaging addition to classroom activities" (panamath.org).

The number sense hasn't only been used for assessment, but has also been the target for intervention. In an early study, Wilson *et al.* (2006) had developed an adaptive computer game-like training program ("The Number Race"; www.thenumberrace.com) and had shown how it improves precision of the number sense.

The number sense as the foundation of mathematical skill: A bridge too far

Despite the elegance of the studies reported above and despite the consistency of the findings across species and research methods, two important questions need to be addressed. First, what is the construct validity of the number sense measure? And second, how can a single factor like the number sense be brought in line with the multifaceted nature of mathematical cognition, with the large individual differences in mathematical skill and heterogeneity of developmental dyscalculia?

Validity of the number sense measure

As indicated above, the number sense task in its basic form presents subjects with two sets of dots that differ in numerosity. Subjects have to indicate which of the two sets contains more dots. The precision with which the numerosity of these two sets can be discriminated is taken as a measure of the acuity of the number sense. Yet, the validity of this measure has been criticised. A serious problem that should be considered is that numerosity correlates with continuous measures like area occupied by the number of dots (more dots occupy more area), total brightness (more white dots have more total white on the screen), density (more dots in a fixed area imply that they are closer together), etcetera. Whatever way the stimuli are constructed, there is no way around this problem: one can control some of these correlating continuous measure but never all of them in the same trial. For instance, one can try to eliminate total area occupied as a cue but this can only be done if one puts the dots close together, thereby increasing density. This leaves the possibility that performance on the number sense task actually does not reflect the accuracy with which numerosity (as countable sets) can be discriminated but rather the efficiency with which these continuous measures can be used as helpful cues (Gebuis & Reynvoet, 2012). Interestingly, this confound between continuous measures and other visual features is not new. As indicated by Gevers et al. (2016; Gebuis et al., 2016), the process of comparing two sets of dots as in the number sense task bears strong similarity with the process of conservation as described by Piaget. A child has to learn that numerosity is independent of physical appearance. In a well-known demonstration two sets of marbles of equal numerosity are put in front of a child in two parallel lines of equal length. The experimenter then takes one set and organises them such that the length of the line increases. The child is then asked which of the two sets contains the most marbles. A child that is not yet able to conserve will indicate that the longer line contains the most marbles (Piaget, 1965). In other words, the child has to learn to inhibit the irrelevant and conflicting visual features. Clearly, this poses serious problems for the nativist idea that performance on the number sense task is based on the biologically old ability to grasp number. Instead, it brings the number sense task in the context of the constructivist idea that the number concept needs to be learned. There is convincing evidence in support of this. First, it has been shown that children below 5 years of age were unable to perform trials with inconsistent features (like more area for the smaller set) (Gebuis et al., 2009; Rousselle, Palmers & Noël, 2004; Soltesz, Szucs & Szucs, 2010). Second, recent work has been able to isolate the process of inhibition of the irrelevant continuous features in the number sense task and has shown that it is this process that correlates with mathematical skill (Gilmore et al., 2013; Bugden & Ansari, 2016). At this point it is not known how exactly the relation between inhibition skill and mathematical skill should be conceived. It is not necessarily the case that it is specifically driven by a true understanding of the number concept. It is also possible that it reflects the more general cognitive control capacity to inhibit the automatic processing of irrelevant information, although some recent research suggests that this may not be the case (Bellon et al., 2016).

Another problem that questions the validity of the nativist number sense idea is that correlation between the number sense measure and arithmetic skill is less strong than originally thought. A recent review has shown that there are more studies that do not show a link between performance in the non-symbolic number sense task than there are studies that do show a link (De Smedt et al., 2013). The link seems to be much stronger for the symbolic version of the number comparison task. This again suggests that it is not the biologically inherited ability to grasp the numerosity of sensory information that forms the core of the development of mathematical skills, but rather that it is the experience with number symbols that is the most important determinant.

In sum, it is clear that the validity of the number sense measure as a predictor of mathematical skill should be approached with a good dose of criticism. There are convincing reasons to believe that it is not the evolutionary old capacity to derive number from sensory information that determines mathematical skill. Although the precise mechanisms are not yet known, the findings suggest that diagnostics, education and remediation should concentrate on other targets, like learning what numbers mean, learning that numerosity should be distinguished from confounding features, learning to concentrate on relevant information and inhibit irrelevant information, facilitating the use of number symbols, learning how they map on numerosity, etc.

Variability in the intraparietal sulcus

As outlined above, one of the important claims of the number sense being foundational to mathematical skill is that the ability to process numerosity resides in a circumscribed region of the brain and that this region of the brain is involved not only in numerosity processing but also in more complex mathematical tasks. Many, if not all brain imaging studies show that the intraparietal sulcus is involved whenever number processing tasks are involved. Yet, there is large variability across studies and tasks with respect to exactly which part of the intraparietal sulcus is involved (see for instance meta-analyses of Cohen Kadosh *et al.*, 2008). The systematicity of this variability is so far not understood. Similarly, at this point, it is not clear whether it is exactly the same brain region that is involved in the processing of non-symbolic numerosity that is also recruited by other tasks like mental arithmetic with symbols. Despite the advances and progress in brain imaging techniques it is extremely difficult to design a study that would allow to draw definite conclusions with respect to the existence of a unique part of the brain that is crucially involved in all number processing tasks and that can be considered to be the neural correlate of the core number sense system. Hence, one should be aware of the fact that the neural involvement of the core number sense hasn't been unequivocally demonstrated, although this is sometimes more or less explicitly suggested and even claimed in the literature. Before this issue is solved it will be impossible to consider neurophysiological or neuroanatomical measures as diagnostic markers for mathematical capacity and skill.

Even simple tasks are supported by more than one brain region

Another important result that is common to most if not all brain imaging studies, but that is often overlooked, is that even the most simple basic number processing tasks that entail not more than comparing two numbers lead to a broad set of activations in the brain. Apparently, even in a simple number comparison task more brain is at work than one single area: dedicated neural processing is needed to translate information impending on the primary visual cortices to activations in the part of the brain that allows this visual stimulation to be recognised as Arabic digits (Shum *et al.*, 2013), from where the neural codes for magnitude representation, i.e. the number sense neural circuitry, in the intraparietal sulcus can be reached. Once this information has been derived, the number magnitude representations need to be compared and transformed into a response, that engages the decision mechanisms of the brain, located in frontal parts of the brain. The integrity of each of these components and the network that they constitute together is a prerequisite for efficient number processing.

Complex tasks need additional components

Considering tasks that are more complex than merely comparing the value of two numbers, the neuroimaging literature has recently highlighted that other key sub-cortical and neocortical brain regions, including inferior frontal gyrus, anterior cingulate gyrus, insula and cerebellum are also systematically related to mathematical cognition tasks (e.g. Arsalidou & Taylor, 2011; Fias *et al.*, 2013). These areas are known to subserve basic neurocognitive functions like language, attention, cognitive control, working memory and executive function. At a broad level of analysis, a number of subsystems can be distinguished. First, the integrity of visual and auditory association cortex which help decode the visual form and phonological features of the stimulus, and the parietal attention system which helps to build semantic representations of quantity. Second, procedural and working memory systems anchored in the basal ganglia and fronto-parietal circuits create short-term representations that support the manipulation of multiple discrete quantities over several seconds. This system also underlies cognitive control systems that optimise performance by monitoring performance, inhibiting undesired responses, etc. Third, episodic and semantic memory systems located in the angular gyrus and hippocampus play an important role in long-term memory formation and generalisation beyond individual problem attributes. Fourth, prefrontal control processes in interaction with the parietal cortex guide and maintain attention in the service of goal-directed decision making.

Generally, it should also be noted that the intraparietal sulcus is involved in the neural circuitry that engages these cognitive functions. Consequently, the involvement of the intraparietal sulcus in a number processing task should not be taken as direct evidence for the involvement of number sense representations. In fact, this would be a prototypical case of reverse inference, which refers to the fact that the functional involvement of a brain region is inferred by that region being active in another region. Especially in the-absence of precise a priori predictions and in the absence of experimental manipulations specifically geared to test these predictions, reverse inference is one of the major pitfalls of brain imaging research (Poldrack, 2006). The intraparietal sulcus is especially vulnerable to this fallacy because it is not a functionally homogenous region (see Menon, 2016) with different parts being differently connected to other brain regions and because it is, as part of association cortex, involved in the neural processing of a wide variety of information.

In sum, given the multi-componential nature of mathematical tasks it is advisable to look at the brain from a network perspective (Fias *et al.*, 2013), thereby giving attention to how brains function as a determinant of behaviour and cognition ultimately is the result of the components of the network and the way they interact. This is of course theoretically more complex than the viewpoint of a single brain region being the core determinant of a cognitive skill, but it offers more opportunity to accommodate the inherent complexity of the phenomena under study and allows for a better understanding of the large individual differences that exist in mathematical development and skill (Desoete, 2015; Kaufmann *et al.*, 2013).

Heterogeneity of developmental dyscalculia

From the assumption of a single core deficit that is responsible for developmental dyscalculia (in casu a deficient number sense), it naturally follows that a substantial degree of homogeneity is predicted in the manifestation of developmental dyscalculia. Of course, some inter individual variation is to be expected as a function of the moment of onset, degree and type of impairment to the number sense, but given the presumed central status of the number sense the consequences of an impairment will be rather uniform. Vice versa, one can predict that the neural basis of developmental dyscalculia and mathematical learning problems can be boiled down to a deficiency of the core neural number sense module, located in the intraparietal sulcus. Using a variety of neuroimaging techniques developmental dyscalculia has been related to various structural and functional brain correlates. It has been found that developmental dyscalculia comes with reduced grey matter volume, reduced white matter connections, deficient brain metabolism and deficient brain function in different parts of the brain, including the intraparietal sulcus but far from exclusively (see Kucian, Kaufmann & Von Aster, 2015 for an overview of these studies). This confirms the picture that many brain regions and their cognitive functions contribute to mathematical cognition.

A related argument that poses serious problems for the number sense view focuses on the prediction of specificity of mathematical learning disorders. If math skill crucially depends on the efficiency of a sole core system that is unique for number processing, then the prediction follows that mathematical skill is quite independent of other cognitive skills. However, this prediction is falsified by the high prevalence of comorbidity of dyscalculia with other learning and developmental disorders like dyslexia, ADHD and developmental dyspraxia. In fact, comorbidities occur way more frequently than is expected on the basis of the prevalence of the individual learning problems. For instance, with an estimated prevalence of 7 per cent for dyscalculia and 7 per cent for dyslexia, one would predict a prevalence of 0.49 per cent if both learning disorders were independent. Yet, in reality comorbidity is more rule than exception with estimates ranging from 25 to 50 per cent of comorbidity for dyscalculia and dyslexia (Landerl & Moll, 2010; Shalev *et al.*, 2000). For dyscalculia and ADHD similar numbers are obtained.

From a theoretical perspective it can be interesting to focus on pure cases of dyscalculia. Indeed, by selecting children who have specific learning problems with numbers one can gain meaningful insight in the consequences and developmental implications of inaccurate number sense representations (e.g. Piazza *et al.*, 2010). Yet, it should always be realised that the possibility to generalise from these observations is limited.

No transfer of number sense training

As indicated above, intervention studies using training programs like the Number Race that focus on the ability to compare numbers have shown that indeed the accuracy of the number representations which are presumed to be the number sense can be improved (Wilson *et al.*, 2006). Yet, contrary to what could be expected from the number sense idea the positive effects that were obtained in number comparison tasks did not convincingly transfer to other types of numerical skill (e.g. Räsänen *et al.*, 2009).

Discussion

Although the above described casus is rather specific to the cognitive neuroscience of numerical and mathematical cognition and may not belong to the core of thinking of early childhood care and education, I believe it nicely illustrates both the possibilities and the limitations of neuroscience research. Cognitive neuroscience is built on strong research methods that allow a scientifically rigorous way of studying the brain in action, thereby allowing empirically based pointers towards the understanding of how our brain determines our psychological constitution. This is nicely illustrated in the ground work that has laid out the neural mechanisms of how numerosity and basic number meaning are neurally encoded. Yet, at the same time the case of the cognitive neuroscience of number also points to the fact that the translation from neuroscience to applied context should always be done with care and in the full awareness that 1) there exist some general societal tendencies that may cause some ideas to receive more attraction than is justified by the facts, and 2) that neuroscience, as any other empirical science, leads to simplification.

What I wanted to draw attention to is that the idea of an inherited number sense as the unique core building block of complex mathematical skill has had an unusual attraction. The exact reason for this attraction is hard to pinpoint. Probably there are multiple contributing factors. To begin with, at first sight the idea has a rich explanatory power: indeed, it encompasses findings in animals and humans alike and fits data obtained at the level of the brain and at the level of behaviour. Second, it fits the general enthusiasm and hope to expect solutions from biological explanations. It seems to be a general tendency of which people aren't always aware of, that neurobiological explanations subjectively seem to have more truth value than merely psychological explanations (Weisberg *et al.*, 2008). Third, and relatedly, the nativist explanation couples the mystery of human mind and behaviour with the promises offered by genetic research and understanding of the genome. The optimism of finding relevant genes, not only for phenomena related to the body but also related to the mind, induced by technological developments in the possibilities for genome sequencing may have induced a bias for relatively simple nativist accounts of complex cognitive skills. Nativist accounts can harvest from this fertile ground. A fourth factor, that may be cause as well as consequence of the two previous possibilities, is the fact that major scientific journals but also the general media relatively easily publish results that are framed in a simple and nativist line of explanation. Findings and studies that focus on the limits of these explanations or more general theoretical frameworks that try to do justice to the complexity and multi-componential nature of the phenomena are published in less impactful and often specialist journals. Therefore, they reach a significantly smaller audience and are less visible and influential.

I want to emphasise that I didn't want to argue that the idea of number sense has no truth value. Understanding number is of course an important aspect of arithmetic and mathematical knowledge, and will in that respect be a cognitive component that meaningfully contributes to mathematical achievement. To have a number sense, i.e. to have a basic understanding of number, is of course meaningful, and I consider what has been achieved so far a major realisation of cognitive neuroscience research, but it shouldn't be forgotten that it is only a small aspect of what mental arithmetic and mathematics is about. A lot of work needs to be done to understand how the basic understanding of number relates to other cognitive skills (like language, executive function, etc.) and how they together allow the more complex levels of mathematical knowledge and skill that our brains are capable of. Relatedly, it is clear that quite some of the building blocks of what we are have an evolutionary history. Hence, the idea of a number sense being inherited is not unlikely at all. Yet, as soon as a child is born, its brain comes into contact with its environment which will also contribute to the development. A lot of work needs to be done to understand the developmental trajectories from basic inherited building block to a matured brain and mind, taking into account how social environment and education have an impact on these developmental trajectories (Kaufmann et al., 2013).

The requirement of experimental control and the constraints intrinsic to the research methods that are used to study the brain will always and unavoidably lead to simplification. Reduction of the complexity of phenomena under study is inherent to neuroscience and necessary to come to scientifically solid understanding of general principles and mechanisms – as it is to other sciences. It is important that this act of reductionism isn't forgotten when translating back to the original phenomena and problems.

Does this mean that we should be pessimistic and give up the idea that neuroscience can meaningfully contribute to understanding phenomena as complex as the development and education of mathematical skill? I don't think so. First, cognitive neuroscience is self-corrective. I hope that my overview of points that have been raised against the idea of an innate number sense as the core determinant of mathematical skill are convincing in this respect. Second, neuroscience is a relatively young science that is still in its infancy. Technology is advancing rapidly with regularly new tools being developed to study different aspects of brain structure and function with increasing precision. For instance, until less than a decade ago, standard brain imaging was mainly restricted to the separate measurement of brain activity in different parts of the brain. In doing so, the brain was studied as a set of independent parts of the brain. Nowadays, however, new techniques and tools have been developed that allow to study the brain as a complex network leading to an increasing understanding of how different parts of the brain communicate and collaborate. To the context of understanding the neural basis of mathematical cognition this opens interesting perspectives, because it will allow to describe and understand the dynamics of how the number sense in the intraparietal sulcus interacts with other parts of the brain that support executive function, etc. Very promising studies have already been published and they begin to unveil how mathematical skill is determined by the strength of connections between brain regions, how mathematical disability can be related to inefficient brain organisation and how this network organisation can be influenced by behavioural remediation programmes (for an overview, see Menon, 2016).

Going back to the basic question of the book, to what extent neuroscience can contribute to early childcare education, I hope that the present case description has illustrated that simple and easy answers are not to be expected from neuroscience. Neuroscience, and cognitive neuroscience in particular, is on the one hand a rapidly and dynamically evolving field of research with new techniques allowing for continuous insight and progress. Yet, on the other hand it comes with the disadvantage that definite and final truths aren't within sight. Accordingly, efforts to translate neuroscience findings and theories need to be flexibly situated in a dynamical changing context.

With respect to the current topic, my position is clearly not that neuroscientific observations shouldn't play a role in thinking about childcare education. To the contrary, I believe it can form an important source of relevant information. Yet, I want to raise the message that it shouldn't be taken as a simplifying factor that provides simple solutions to complex problems. The hopeful aspect of recent developments in neuroscience is that there is the development towards systems neuroscience that treats the brain as a complex system. In principle, this allows the construction of a knowledge base that has the capacity to deal with the complexity that is inherent to childcare. But even then, one should realise that the match between neuroscience and early childhood care and education will always be approximate. Meaningful and useful links can only be made in the context of other scientific disciplines, especially when the strengths and weaknesses of these disciplines are complementary.

References

Agrillo, C., Dadda, M., & Bisazza, A. (2007). Quantity discrimination in female mosquitofish. *Animal Cognition*, 10(1), 63–70.

Arsalidou, M., & Taylor, M. J. (2011). Is 2+2=4? Meta-analyses of brain areas needed for numbers and calculations. *NeuroImage*, 54(4), 2382–2393.

Bellon, E., Fias, W., & De Smedt, B. (2016). Are individual differences in arithmetic fact retrieval in children related to inhibition? *Frontiers in Psychology*, 7, 825.

Bugden, S., & Ansari, D. (2016). Probing the nature of deficits in the 'Approximate Number System' in children with persistent developmental dyscalculia. *Developmental Science*, 19(5), 817–833.

Butterworth, B. (2005). The development of arithmetical abilities. *Journal of Child Psychology and Psychiatry*, 46(1), 3–18.

Cantlon, J. F., Brannon, E. M., Carter, E. J., & Pelphrey, K. A. (2006). Functional imaging of numerical processing in adults and 4-y-old children. *PLoS Biology*, 4(5), e125.

Cohen Kadosh, R., Lammertyn, J., & Izard, V. (2008). Are numbers special? An overview of chronometric, neuroimaging, developmental and comparative studies of magnitude representation. *Progress in Neurobiology*, 84(2), 132–147.

Davis, H., & Perusse, R. (1988). Numerical competence in animals: Definitional issues, current evidence, and a new research agenda. *Behavioral and Brain Sciences*, 11(4), 561–615.

De Smedt, B., Noël, M.-P., Gilmore, C., & Ansari, D. (2013). How do symbolic and non-symbolic numerical magnitude processing skills relate to individual differences in children's mathematical skills? A review of evidence from brain and behavior. *Trends in Neuroscience and Education*, 2(2), 48–55.

Desoete, A. (2015). Cognitive predictors of mathematical abilities and disabilities. In R. Cohen Kadosh and A. Dowker (Eds.), *The oxford handbook of numerical cognition*. Oxford: Oxford University Press.

Devlin, K. (2005). *The math instinct: Why you're a mathematical genius (along with lobsters, birds, cats, and dogs)*. New York: Thunder's Mouth Press.

Fias, W., Menon, V., & Szucs, D. (2013). Multiple components of developmental dyscalculia. *Trends in Education and Neuroscience*, 2(2), 43–47.

Gebuis, T., & Reynvoet, B. (2012). The interplay between nonsymbolic number and its continuous visual properties. *Journal of Experimental Psychology*, 141(4), 642–648.

Gebuis, T., Cohen Kadosh, R., & Gevers, W. (2016). Sensory-integration system rather than approximate number system underlies numerosity processing: A critical review. *Acta Psychologica*, 171, 17–35.

Gebuis, T., Cohen Kadosh, R., de Haan, E., & Henik, A. (2009). Automatic quantity processing in 5-year olds and adults. *Cognitive Processing*, 10(2), 133–142.

Gevers, W., Cohen Kadosh, R., & Gebuis, T. (2016). The sensory integration theory: An alternative to the approximate number system. In A. Henik (Ed.), *Continuous issues in numerical cognition*. San Diego: Academic Press.

Gilmore, C., Attridge, N., Clayton, S., Cragg, L., Johnson, S., Marlow, N., … Inglis, M. (2013). Individual differences in inhibitory control, not non-verbal number acuity, correlate with mathematics achievement. *PLoS ONE*, 8(6), e67374.

Halberda, J., Mazzocco, M. M. M., & Feigenson, L. (2008). Individual differences in non-verbal number acuity correlate with maths achievement. *Nature*, 455, 665–668.

Hyde, D. C., & Spelke, E. S. (2011). Neural signatures of number processing in human infants: Evidence for two core systems underlying non-verbal numerical cognition. *Developmental Science*, 14(2), 360–371.

Izard, V., Sann, C., Spelke, E. S., & Streri, A. (2009). Newborn infants perceive abstract numbers. *Proceedings of the National Academy of Sciences*, 106(25), 10382–10385.

Kaufmann, L., Mazzocco, M. M., Dowker, A., Von Aster, M., Göbel, S. M., Grabner, R. H., Henik, A., Jordan, N. C., Karmiloff-Smith, A. D., Kucian, K., Rubinsten, O., Szucs, D., Shalev, R., & Nuerk, H. C. (2013). Dyscalculia from a developmental and differential perspective. *Frontiers in Psychology*, 4, 516.

Kucian, K., Kaufmann, L., & Von Aster, M. (2015). Brain correlates of numerical disabilities. In R. Cohen Kadosh and A. Dowker (Eds.), *The oxford handbook of numerical cognition*. Oxford: Oxford University Press.

Landerl, K., & Moll, K. (2010). Comorbidity of learning disorders: Prevalence and familial transmission. *Journal of Child Psychology and Psychiatry and Allied Disciplines*, 51, 287–294.

Menon, V. (2016). Memory and cognitive control circuits in mathematical cognition and learning. In M. Cappelletti and W. Fias (Eds.), *The mathematical brain across the life span* (159–186). Progress in Brain Research, Vol. 227. Amsterdam: Elsevier.

Nieder, A., & Miller, E. K. (2004). A parieto-frontal network for visual numerical information in the monkey. *Proceedings of the National Academy of Sciences*, 101(19), 7457–7462.

Piaget, J. (1965). *The child's conception of number.* New York: W. Norton Company & Inc.

Piazza, M., Facoetti, A., Trussardi, A. N., Berteletti, I., Conte, S., Lucangeli, D., Dehaene, S., & Zorzi, M. (2010). Developmental trajectory of number acuity reveals a severe impairment in developmental dyscalculia. *Cognition*, 116(1), 33–41.

Poldrack, R. A. (2006). Can cognitive processes be inferred from neuroimaging data? *Trends in Cognitive Sciences*, 10(2), 59–63.

Räsänen, P., Salminen, J., Wilson, A. J., Aunio, P., & Dehaene, S. (2009). Computer-assisted intervention for children with low numeracy skills. *Cognitive Development*, 24(4), 450–472.

Ritchie, S. J., & Bates, T. C. (2013). Enduring links from childhood mathematics and reading achievement to adult socioeconomic status. *Psychological Science*, 24(7), 1301–1308.

Rousselle, L., Palmers, E., & Noël, M. P. (2004). Magnitude comparison in preschoolers: What counts? Influence of perceptual variables. *Journal of Experimental and Child Psychology*, 87(1), 57–84.

Santens, S., Roggeman, C., Fias, W., & Verguts, T. (2010). Number processing pathways in human parietal cortex. *Cerebral Cortex*, 20(1), 77–88.

Shalev, R. S., Auerbach, J., Manor, O., & Gross-Tsur, V. (2000). Developmental dyscalculia: Prevalence and prognosis. *European Child and Adolescent Psychiatry*, 9(Suppl 2), II58–64. Available at: http://www.ncbi.nlm.nih.gov/pubmed/11138905.

Shum, J., Hermes, D., Foster, B. L., Dastjerdi, M., Rangarajan, V., Winawer, J., Miller, K. J., & Parvizi, J. (2013). A brain area for visual numerals. *Journal of Neuroscience*, 33(16), 6709–6715.

Soltesz, F., Szucs, D., & Szucs, L. (2010). Relationships between magnitude representation, counting and memory in 4- to 7-year-old children: A developmental study. *Behavioral and Brain Functions*, 6(13), 1–14.

Weisberg, D. S., Keil, F. C., Goodstein, J., Rawson, E., & Gray, J. R. (2008). The seductive allure of neuroscience explanations. *Journal of Cognitive Neuroscience*, 20(3), 470–477.

Wilson, A. J., Revkin, S. K., Cohen, D., Cohen, L., & Dehaene, S. (2006). An open trial assessment of 'The Number Race', an adaptive computer game for remediation of dyscalculia. *Behavioral and Brain Functions*, 2(1), 20.

DISCUSSION

Michel Vandenbroeck and Liselott Mariett Olsson

As Rose and Rose (2016) pointed out: neuro is the proliferating prefix. It seems to be everywhere in early childhood care and education. Several contributors in this book have illustrated the proliferation of the neuro-discourse by quoting governmental texts, the Allen (2011) and Field (2010) reports being distinct examples, just as the publications from the Worldbank. This may lead to the impression that the use of neuroscience in early childhood education is first and foremost a matter of (neo)liberal governments. That impression would, however, create a false dichotomy between the state and civil society. Foucault (1990) warned us not to dwell in such false antagonisms that afflict the notion of "state" with a pejorative connotation while idealising "civil society" as a good, living, warm whole. Indeed, the erroneous use of the neuro-language in early childhood education is by far not the monopoly of science or governmental bodies. There are many examples to illustrate how civil society is permeated by the same narratives of the Allen and Field reports and, consequently, of the social investment and econometric paradigms.

Eurochild (2015: 5) for example speaks about a "child centred investment strategy". They make explicit reference to the Harvard Center on the Developing Child, stating that "A growing body of neuro-science points to the critical importance of the first five years of a child's life in brain development. ... Conversely, if a child misses out on a stimulating and nurturing environment in the early years, it can be difficult to catch up and can negatively affect life-time chances." Save the Children (Finnegan & Lawton, 2016) quotes the National Scientific Council on the Developing Child to also tell the story about synapto-genesis and critical periods. They argue that by age 3, a child's brain is estimated to be twice as active as an adult's brain and that at the same time, the rapid growth in the size of a child's brain and in the formation of synapses begin to slow. Their publication makes use of colourful images to depict how language circuits in the brain change during childhood and they give "top tips for parents" on how "you can help build your child's brain by talking to them right from the start". The critical period narrative is ultimately used as a plea for investing more public funds in nurseries.

This is also the case of UNICEF. The title of their 2014 symposium "The Three Pound Universe" is eloquent, and in their publications (e.g. UNICEF, 2014a; 2014b) they go with the story that early intervention is the answer, because it becomes progressively harder to fix problems later in life.

Similarly, UNESCO has also taken over the discourse, including the specific vocabulary that the framing agencies proposed to influence policies (see Shonkoff and Bales, 2011). UNESCO (2012) writes about "the child's brain *architecture*" that is *"wired* in the first five years of life", they also took over the terms of "chronic unrelenting stress in early childhood, caused by extreme poverty" and the concept of sensitive, if not critical, periods of brain development, using similar pictures (Council for Early Child Development, 2010 in UNESCO, 2012) than those that are criticised by Sue White and Dave Wastell in their contribution to this book. In many of these publications by NGOs the neuroscience is used as an argument to claim considerable "returns on investment", either directly (you will save money later on) or indirectly (it will cost you a lot if you repair rather than prevent). The use of neuroscience along with an economic investment rationale in early childhood education is also to be noticed in local interventions, evenings for parents, and discussions between private day care organisers and local authorities (Boyle, 2016). It is impossible to know to what extent the use of neuroscience to gain political attention for one's objectives is based on the belief that one attaches to the claims of lobby groups such as the Harvard Center on the Developing Child, or to what extent that is just a façade, because one assumes that other – moral, ethical or rights based – claims do not stand a chance in these neoliberal times. It is not only impossible to know; it is also irrelevant. The effect is entirely the same: it is as if all agree that there is but one rational for publicly funding early childhood care and education: the alleged economic benefits. And in so doing, NGOs and local activists risk making their crucial place in the democratic public debate – as crucial part of the civil society – redundant.

It is clear that the neuro-turn, together with this economic language of investments, and what White and Wastell have ironised as Outcomes Theology is not just a matter of policy makers alone, but can be labelled as a dominant discourse in the Foucauldian sense: a story that is so dominant that thinking about children and early childhood in different ways becomes very difficult (Foucault, 1966). The many examples of how this discourse has not only permeated civil society but has also been shaped by local NGOs and social workers and early years educators in the field (Boyle, 2016) clearly show that policy is not the monopoly of policy makers and practice is not to be reduced to policy that trickled down. On a positive note, this means that discourse can also be contested bottom up, as well as top down. Or in the words of Foucault, dominant discourse always goes hand in hand with resistance (Pickett, 1996).

Translating neuroscience into education

The contributions in this book illustrate how we should be cautious when referring to these narratives. On August 13, 2016, well-known neuroscientist Max Coltheart tweeted: "At present, there are no findings from neuroscience that have implications for classroom practice." He is immediately acknowledged by Professor Anne Castles of the Department of Cognitive Science, Macquarie University: "Most definitely!"

That is not to say that neuroscience is – and for ever will be – useless for education and neuroscientists are optimistic that somewhere in the future, their science will have evolved to a stage where it may be able to give some advice about education. Wim Fias shares this optimism, claiming that neuroscience is self-correcting and still very young a science. As a neuroscientist, he sketched the possibilities and the limitations of neuroscientific research and their relation to educational purposes. Yet he seriously warns us for simplistic conclusions.

Through the case of number processing, he gave a detailed insiders' view on the transformation of robust scientific results in dominant narratives that are attractive and simple, but lack evidence to support them. His plea for "a good dose of criticism" when it comes to constructing validity and even more so when it comes to translating neuroscience in education is important. It should indeed be noted that much of the claims about translating brain research in educational practice or policy are not made by neuroscientists, often much to the distaste of the brain researchers themselves. It is probably not a coincidence that some of the more severe criticisms on the use of brain research in the field of early childhood care and education come from (former or present) neuroscientists, such as Raymond Tallis (2013), Hillary and Steven Rose (2012; 2016), or indeed Dave Wastell (Wastell & White, 2012) who contributed to this book. Many of their arguments relate to the yet unknown complexity and plasticity of the brain and to what Wim Fias calls the brain as a network.

The contributions of Helen Penn, Sue White and Dave Wastell in this book deplore that the necessary caution and critical self-correcting attitude is scarce when neuroscience is translated into educational and social policy. As they rightly claim: evidence does not speak for itself, it has to be spoken for. Images of parts of the brain that appear to "light up" cannot self-evidently be translated in educational or social policies. Nor can animal research be directly translated to the growth of the baby brain. In between stand theories and conceptions of the human nature, ideas about what a society needs, ideologies about parental responsibility and the role of the state, and – ultimately – an image of what a child is. Through many examples (the case of non-consensual adoption being a particularly salient and worrying one) they illustrate that all too often the neuroscience is limited to "materialise" what was already known, yet used for political aims that are way beyond the evidence produced, a critical claim also made by Ramaekers and Suissa (2012). As Penn has illustrated, this materialisation (e.g. "the brain is an organ that develops in the same way for all children") is also a naturalisation and thus inherently a far-reaching decontextualisation. This way of using brain research leads to universal claims and remedies, ignoring cultural preferences, political histories and social contexts, and *a fortiori* ignoring the local voices of parents and practitioners on what early childhood education is for or what is desirable.

Translating neuroscience into the political

Equally important than the question of what is true is the question of what is desirable (Biesta, 2007). As Helen Penn rightly argued in chapter 4, highly specialised and highly limited findings cannot be extrapolated to make general prescriptions about policy. Indeed, contrary to the plea of Shonkoff and Leavitt (2010), linking neuroscience to early childhood policy and moving from *why* to *what and how* is anything but straightforward. Indeed, policy – and even more so the political (Mouffe, 2005) – is about what constitutes the good life, about what is desirable. And what is considered desirable cannot just be derived from what is considered true. Between science and policy lie ethical and moral opinions about social justice, about what is fair, ideas on what constitutes human dignity and on what is democracy. Obviously – and very luckily – these opinions and ideas are far from consensual. Citizens may deeply disagree on these questions and that disagreement is vital as it forms the core of what Mouffe (2005) calls the political, without which there would be no democracy.

The unique contribution of Jan De Vos in this book goes even further, by challenging the claim in the introduction that this book is about the use of neuroscience and not about neuroscience itself and by analysing the relations between neurologization, medicalisation, psychologization and – crucially – digitalisation. His analysis is not to be reduced to a mere (somewhat outdated) fear of Big Brother, but he gives us food for critical thought about how the image of the child (as well as the image of Man) has indeed changed in present-day neoliberal times. He draws our attention to the warnings of Hannah Arendt on the problematic relation between Truth and Policy, between the conceptualisation of human activity and what is desirable.

In neoliberalism it seems that the question of what is desirable is beyond discussion: what is desirable is what is profitable. What is desirable is what supports economic growth. And that is a matter of individual freedom and individual responsibility in a competitive and meritocratic system where one "earns what one deserves". It is assumed that the market is inherently fair and that assumption dismisses ethical concerns about inequality and solidarity.

And into early childhood policies

The prevalence of the neuroscientific narrative in early childhood education does indeed not come alone. It is accompanied by its inseparable twin brother: the narrative on the social investment state, on the return on investments, on human capital. As Penn noted, this notion of human capital has profoundly shifted from the *humane* human capital of Amartya Sen to the neoliberal concept of human capital assuming self-conscious, self-supportive individuals who are responsible for their own development and prosperity. And thus, the neuro-discourse and its human capital twin brother go hand in hand with an image of the child as what it is yet to become: an autonomous, entrepreneurial citizen, anything but dependent on the state (Masschelein, 2001; Ramaekers & Suissa, 2012). The image of the child as a cost (be it a profitable one) and as what it has yet to become reduces education to the preparation for later life and thus reduces the meaning of early childhood education to a preparation for compulsory education (Moss, 2013), which is – in turn – reduced to a preparation for the labour market. In such a world view, there is only limited space for interdependency, collaboration, solidarity, fairness, democracy and care, concepts that were so dear to generations of pedagogues, including Dewey (1916), Freinet (1929), Freire (1970), Malaguzzi (Cagliari *et al.*, 2016) and many others.

Neoliberal conceptions of the welfare state have given momentum to more meritocratic conceptions of fairness or social justice, that indeed moved away from the more solidaristic notions that prevailed in times of educational reforms under these inspiring pedagogues. It has been well documented how the welfare state evolved in a more contractual welfare state and equality of opportunity has replaced the equality of outcomes as a principle of fairness (Morabito, Vandenbroeck & Roose, 2013). Jan De Vos explained how intra-individual concepts (i.e. empathy) risk to decontextualise the socio-economical and the political, occluding issues such as inequality and power relations. Sue White, Dave Wastell and Helen Penn have documented in their contributions that the focus on the early years and the very concept of critical (or sensitive) periods give a scientific rationale to the shift of the equilisandum from outcomes to opportunities. As the neuroscience is believed to be beyond doubt, and no one can object that it is better to prevent than to cure, the meritocratic individualising discourse on poverty, blaming the victim, is silently and gradually also accepted. This meritocratic discourse implies that poverty is an individual responsibility and that (early childhood) education rather than redistribution is the solution. In this vein, one can see that naming "poverty" as the problem and "poverty reduction" as the solution is of course already a framing of the problem that would benefit from a broader discussion. One could indeed, as Wilkinson and Pickett (2009) and Picketty (2014) do, argue that it is not poverty that is the main problem, but inequality, and that therefore poverty reduction cannot exist without the reduction of wealth and thus redistributive policies. These are just a few examples of discussions that risk to remain covered in the absence of a plurality of discourses and that illustrate how education cannot be understood without its social, ethical and political contexts.

Precisely because the use of neuroscience is so inextricably intertwined with the eminently political and ethical discourse on social investment and return on investment, it is extremely worrying that these narratives have permeated in local and international NGOs and the wider civil society. In their quest for the just causes (such as education for all) they make use of the economic argument in order to have their voices heard by those who decide where to invest their money. Yet, in so doing, they reinforce the idea that the only valuable argument is an economic one and that spending public money in early childhood education can only be justified by its later return on investments. In so doing, the civil society would indeed converge with Foucault's warning not to dichotomise state and civil society, as they would contribute to the devaluation of ethical, moral and social concerns in political decision making.

Practice as policy and science

Several of the pedagogues mentioned in the previous paragraph have considered education as inherently democratic. Some framed education as a means to do justice to specific populations such as labourers in Brazil (Freire) or farmers' and labour class children in France (Freinet). Others have considered education as one of the means to restore democracy after fascism (Malaguzzi). They have in common that what happens in daily practice (arrangements of space, relations with families, activities of children, …) is related to one's vision of society, of education and thus of the very meaning of the educational system. In short, one cannot distinguish practice from policy or science. This is also clear in the case of the neuro-discourse. The univocal focus on the early years as preventive of later harm (i.e. developmental delays) has led to a search for evidence-based programmes, what White and Wastell denounce as a spectacular case of the tail wagging the dog. These educational programmes are expected to generate predefined outcomes, without necessarily questioning the desirability of these outcomes with those who are concerned: children, parents, communities and – of course – the professionals of early childhood education (Biesta, 2007). A salient example of this is the International Early Learning Study (IELS) of the OECD (2015). Its ambition is to measure early learning outcomes in the domains of cognitive, social and emotional skills. The study is tendered to be implemented without any concertation of the early childhood professionals in the countries that are concerned (Moss et al., 2016). The danger is indeed that in doing so, the very meaning of early childhood education – and thus the daily practice – is decided without discussion with the direct stakeholders. Another danger is that objectives that do not fall under these developmental outcomes are ignored, despite their prominent place in curricula from New Zealand and Berlin (e.g. the attention for dealing with societal diversity), Belgium (the attention for how child care may influence social cohesion) and many other countries. The programmes reduce the act of education to a technical procedure, i.e. the application of some general and universal rules (e.g. serve and return), and, in doing so, the pedagogue him- or herself becomes a technical professional. Yet care is not a technical matter, and one cannot expect pedagogues to take care if they are not taken care of. In her PhD research, Katrien Van Laere (Van Laere & Vandenbroeck, 2016) conducted focus groups with many parents and professionals about how they make meaning of education and care in Belgian preschool. Discussions about the meaning of pre-school are reduced to the importance of early learning and professionals can hardly legitimise their desire to also care for the children. Meanwhile, parents concur with that discourse, but ask one additional question: will you love my child?

The discussion is of course not to replace one hegemonic discourse (be it a meritocratic) by another single voice. It is rather to say with John Dewey (who in turn quoted Lincoln's Gettysburg Address) that democracy is simply "the government of the people, for the people and by the people" (Dewey, 1916: 303) and can therefore not be dictated by science, nor can it be univocal: "To the educator for whom the problems of democracy are at all *real*, the vital necessity appears to be that of making the connection between the child and his environment as complete and intelligent as possible, both for the welfare of the child and for the sake of the community. The way this is to be accomplished will, of course, *vary according to the conditions of the community*" (p. 289, emphasis added).

Transforming neuroscience, policy and politics through early childhood care and education

Indeed, it is a question of whether we should consider the problems of democracy in early childhood education and care as *real* problems, rather than obeying the current "abstract formalism" (Løvlie, 2007) that surrounds early childhood. This abstract formalism is the very logic that ties together a preference for "interiority" (development and learning takes place *within* each individual) with the desire for control (standards and accountability movements) and the longing for measureable results (economic investment in "early intervention" and the child as "human capital"). As shown in the introduction to this book, this is not something specific to neuroscience and it is not entirely new. Psychology and more specifically developmental psychology was the forerunner and it has had a long-lasting impact on early childhood education. What this book and all its contributors show is that this logic of abstract formalism and the unqualified application of the neuroscientific paradigm in early childhood education might be but yet another attempt of abstraction of *real* people, *real* practices and *real* lives in early childhood care and education.

So, what to do in this current situation? Maybe what is needed is a little bit less of historical obliviousness and a little bit more of eagerness to (re)turn to, but also (re)invent history. Because what is then originally and *really* early childhood education about? The significant Greek origin of education (*scholê*) took place at a place – distinct from both the city-state (*polis*) and the household (*oikos*) – and made possible the study of the world, the formation of knowledge into "common goods" and new generations' renewal of society. Education here had "the *potential* to give everyone, regardless of background, natural talent or aptitude, the time and space to leave their known environment, rise above themselves and renew (and thus change in unpredictable ways) the world" (Masschelein & Simons, 2013: 12). Within this definition of education, the focus is not so much on the individual child but rather on the very place of education, the time and space needed to study the world. It is not about "interiority", quite on the contrary it is about the outside – the world and the possibility of studying the world and relating to that world. Neither is it primarily about results – and certainly not about pre-defined and measureable results – as it invites and creates conditions for new generations' *renewal* of society. What is focused here is the *relation* between the child and the world. Just as Dewey claims in the quote above it is "making the connection between the child and his environment as complete and intelligent as possible" that is of importance. That is, in an educational context it is not of interest whether brains in themselves are intelligent or not. Rather it is the relation between child and environment in itself that needs to be made complete and intelligent. Moreover, for Dewey in the quote above, the successful making of complete and intelligent connections between the child and its environment is beneficial both for the child and for the community. It is the very openness in this continuously transforming relation between individual and society that for Dewey assures democracy as "the government of the people, for the people and by the people". This implies that the everyday work in early childhood practices is *really* about assuring the continuous democratic process of simultaneously *studying and renewing* the world. Any teacher, or for that matter anyone that comes into contact with very young children, has the difficult task of creating the conditions – offering and setting up time and space – where this vital and transformative relation between child and world can happen.

Pedagogy is not applied psychology

Tools for relating the child to the social environment cannot be found in any scientific discipline that focuses only on individuals, interiority, control and results. Any attempts to, within such logic, create any kind of pedagogy – including "neuropedagogy" – becomes nothing more than an oxymoron. Such efforts become impossible because they don't even account for half of the relation that defines it as a pedagogical and educational phenomenon. Of course, there are many disciplines that offer knowledge that can help us to direct our educational efforts. Developmental psychologists have historically informed us, and continue to do so, on how children acquire knowledge, on how the child's experimentation is driving it to new insights (e.g. Piaget, 1975), and how this learning in inherently relational (e.g. Stambak *et al.*, 1983), but also culturally defined (e.g. Bruner, 1996; Rogoff *et al.*, 2005). Health sciences have also much contributed to our understanding of the relations between mind and body. Neuroscientists will undoubtedly be able to make substantial contributions to our knowledge base about how the environment influences our brain activity. Yet pedagogy will also be concerned with the questions of education for what?

As indicated in the preface to this book, tools for making time and space for vital and transformative relations between child and world can be found precisely within pedagogical and educational theories that historically have given consistency to educational practices. There is also a rich array of philosophical and aesthetical perspectives that – rather than obeying the logic of abstract formalism – consider educational experiences and events as taking place in a processual and contextual whole and as intimately connected to the material conditions and resources that the very time and space for education offer. Dewey, for instance, talks about experience as not pertaining to an individual, but rather to the situation, the "story" or the "plot" itself, that demands "a stage, a space, wherein to develop and time in which to unfold" (Dewey, 1934: 42). French philosophers Gilles Deleuze and Félix Guattari (2004) for their part, replace the individual with concepts, such as "assemblages", containing both human and non-human matter that find themselves in continuous processes of becoming. Feminist corporeal-materialist aesthetics, as described by art theoretician Marsha Meskimmon, in turn, "challenges conventional concepts of subjectivity, moves away from representation and helps to rethink agency" (Meskimmon, 2016: 1). Agency here is not pertaining to the individual subject, but is seen as "an action" (ibid). This perspective further shows how bodies and spaces mutually define each other and through notions such as "figuration", the embedded and positioned subject is acknowledged at the same time as it promotes a vision of both material space and the subject as dynamic and transforming entities. This is, then, a different conception of *real* than the one presented to us within current abstract formalism in education. Reality is here being given status and modus as material but still continuously transforming and it is "a thinking-in making that matters" (Meskimmon, 2016: 6). All of these seem to us to be very fruitful theoretical tools for contesting current abstract formalism, but they are also tools that seem capable of letting early childhood education and care take place through *action* at place. So, it is not only that we are *confined to* visions of education that shape practices, it is also that early childhood practices can – and already do – *transform* visions of education through practical work.

We should therefore also take into account *real* children's possibilities to inform and transform current abstract formalism in early childhood education and care. As noted by Helen Penn, the ones concerned are as flagrantly lacking with their presence as the very invisibility of the grey matter that has come to so matter in early childhood education and care. Children, even at a very young age, do enter many of the problems and questions that the world presents us with, bodies and brains included. A 4-year-old child once said to us during a discussion on "having ideas": "All my ideas come about as I am working, I have all my ideas in my hands, I think through my hands." Now, this expression clearly demonstrates (might even be considered *evidence* of) that children not only have ideas worth listening to, but also that they have *ideas of ideas* that might be worth taking into account. In our continuing work with this *Childhood* series we will make an effort to pay attention to all the counter-effectuations that the ones concerned – *real* children, teachers, families – readily and continuously perform in early childhood education and care.

Upcoming books in the series will, for instance, bring forward notions of the public early childhood teacher, of the aesthetic dimension of education, of space and place – including material/immaterial tools such as new technologies – all essential issues for early childhood practices. We will (re)turn to and (re)invent central historical pedagogical figures and we will not only continue contesting but also continue to present alternatives to the current abstract formalism in early childhood education and care.

So, "stay tuned", there is more to come.

References

Allen, G. (2011). *Early intervention: Smart investment, massive savings.* The second independent report to Her Majesty's Government. London: HM Government.

Biesta, G. (2007). Why "What Works" won't work: Evidence-based practice and the democratic deficit in educational research. *Educational Theory*, 57(1), 1–22.

Boyle, C. (2016). Key discourses in early childhood intervention: A case study of an early intervention city. Unpublished PhD thesis. Belfast: Queen's University.

Bruner, J. (1996). *The culture of education.* Cambridge, MA: Harvard University Press.

Cagliari, P., Castagnetti, M., Giudici, C., Rinaldi, C., Vecchi, V., & Moss, P. (2016). *Loris Malaguzzi and the schools of Reggio Emilia.* London: Routledge.

Deleuze, G., & Guattari, F. (2004). *A thousand plateaus: Capitalism and schizophrenia.* London: Continuum.

Dewey, J. (1916). *Democracy and education: An introduction to the philosophy of education.* New York: Macmillan.

Dewey, J. (1980 [1934]). *Art as experience.* New York: Perigee Books.

Eurochild (2015). *A child-centred investment strategy: Why the investment plan for Europe needs to prioritise children.* Brussels: Eurochild AISBL.

Field, F. (2010). *The foundation years: Preventing poor children becoming poor adults. The report of the independent review on poverty and life chances.* London: HM Government.

Finnegan, J., & Lawton, K. (2016). Lighting up young brains: How parents, carers and nurseries support children's brain development in the first five years. Retrieved from http://www.savethechildren.org.uk/sites/default/files/images/Lighting_Up_Young_Brains1_0CSCupdate.pdf.

Foucault, M. (1966). *Les mots et les choses.* Paris: Gallimard.

Foucault, M. (1990). *Politics, philosophy, culture. Interviews and other writings 1977–1984.* London: Routledge.

Freinet, C. (1929). Notes de pédagogie révolutionnaire: Les coöpératives scolaires. *Ecole Emancipée*, 31, 506–507.

Freire, P. (1970). *Pedagogy of the oppressed.* New York: Herder and Herder.

Løvlie, L. (2007). The pedagogy of place. *Nordisk Pedagogik*, 27(1), 32–37

Masschelein, J. (2001). The discourse of the learning society and the loss of childhood. *Journal of Philosophy of Education*, 35(1), 1–20.

Masschelein, J., & Simons, M. (2013). *In defence of the school. A public issue.* Leuven: E-ducation Culture & Society Publishers.

Meskimmon, M. (2016) Art matters: Feminist corporeal-materialist aesthetics. In H. Robinson & M. E. Buszek (Ed.) *The companion to feminist art practice and theory.* Oxford: Wiley Blackwell.

Morabito, C., Vandenbroeck, M., & Roose, R. (2013). "The greatest of equalisers": A critical review of international organisations' views on early childhood care and education. *Journal of Social Policy*, 42(3), 451–467.

Moss, P. (2013). The relationship between early childhood and compulsory education: A properly political question. In P. Moss (Ed.), *Early childhood and compulsory education: Reconceptualising the relationship.* London: Routledge.

Moss, P., Dahlberg, G., Grieshaber, S., Mantovani, S., May, H., Pence, A., … Vanden-broeck, M. (2016). The organisation for economic co-operation and development's international early learning study: Opening for debate and contestation. *Contemporary Issues in Early Childhood*, 17(3), 343–351.

Mouffe, C. (2005). *On the political*. London: Routledge.

OECD (2015). Call for tenders: International early learning study. Retrieved from http://www.oecd.org/callsfortenders/CfT%20100001420%20International%20Early%20Lea rning%20Study.pdf.

Piaget, J. (1975). *L'équilibration des structures cognitives*. Paris: Presses Universitaires de France.

Pickett, B. L. (1996). Foucault and the politics of resistance. *Polity*, 28(4), 445–466.

Picketty, T. (2014). *Capital in the twenty-first century*. Cambridge, MA: Harvard University Press.

Ramaekers, S., & Suissa, J. (2012). *The claims of parenting. Reasons, responsibility and society*. Dordrecht, Heidelberg, London, New York: Springer.

Rogoff, B., Moore, L., Najafi, B., Dexter, A., Correa-Chàvez, M., & Solis, J. (2005). Children's development of cultural repertoires through participation in everyday routines and practices. In J. Grusec & P. Hastings (Eds.), *Handbook of socialization*. New York: Guilford.

Rose, H., & Rose, S. (2012). *Genes, cells and brains: The Promethean promises of the new biology*. London: Verso.

Rose, H., & Rose, S. (2016). *Can neuroscience change our minds?* Malden: Polity Press.

Shonkoff, J. P., & Leavitt, P. (2010). Neuroscience and the future of early childhood policy: Moving from why to what and how. *Neuron*, 67(5), 689–691.

Shonkoff, J. P., & Bales, S. N. (2011). Science does not speak for itself: Translating child development research for the public and its policymakers. *Child Development*, 82(1), 17–32.

Stambak, M., Barrière, M., Bonica, L., & Maisonnet, R. (1983). *Les bébés entre eux: Découvrir, jouer, inventer ensemble*. Paris: Presses Universitaires de France.

Tallis, R. (2013). Think brain scans can reveal our innermost thoughts? Think again. June 2, *The Observer*.

UNICEF (2014a). *Early childhood development: A statistical snapshot. Building better brains and sustainable outcomes for children*. New York: UNICEF.

UNICEF (2014b). *Building better brains. New frontiers in early childhood development*. New York: UNICEF.

United Nations Educational Scientific and Cultural Organization (UNESCO) (2012). Early childhood care and education. Presentation at the 2012 EFA Global Action Week. New York: UNESCO.

Van Laere, K., & Vandenbroeck, M. (2016). The (in)convenience of care in preschool education: Examining staff views on Educare. *Early Years*. Retrieved from http://dx.doi.org/10.1080/09575146.2016.1252727.

Wastell, D., & White, S. (2012). Blinded by neuroscience social policy, the family and the infant brain. *Families, Relationships and Societies*, 1(3), 399–416.

Wilkinson, R., & Pickett, K. (2009). *The spirit level: Why more equal societies almost always do better*. Toronto: Allen Lane.

INDEX